ROSES
IN
GARDENS

Formal rose beds on the grand scale, beautifully set off by well-kept lawns.
(Opposite) A traditional brick and timber pergola supporting 'Chaplin's Pink' and other old climbers.

· GARDENING · BY · DESIGN ·

ROSES
IN
GARDENS

· ALAN · TOOGOOD ·

Ward Lock Limited · London

ACKNOWLEDGEMENTS

The publishers are grateful to the following for granting permission to reproduce the following colour photographs: Bob Challinor (pp 10, 11, 14, 15, 50, 62 & 63); and R.C. Balfour Esq. (back cover and pp 3, 42, 43, 46, 47, 55, 58, 59 & 67). The front cover photograph and the photograph on p 22 were taken by Bob Challinor; the photographs on pp 2, 18, 19, 23, 30, 31, 34, 35, 38, 39, 51 & 66 were taken by John Heseltine.

The publishers are especially grateful to the following garden owners for allowing us to photograph their gardens: Christopher Lloyd (p 30); Mr and Mrs D. Simmons (front cover); and The Royal National Rose Society (various).

All the line drawings were drawn by Nils Solberg.

© Ward Lock Ltd 1987

First published in Great Britain in 1987
by Ward Lock Limited, 8 Clifford Street
London W1X 1RB, an Egmont Company

House editor Denis Ingram

Text set in Bembo Roman
by HBM Typesetting Limited, Chorley, Lancashire

Printed and bound in France by Brodard

British Library Cataloguing in Publication Data
Toogood, Alan R.
  Roses in gardens.
  1. Roses
  I. Title
  635.9'33372 SB411

ISBN 0-7063-6540-2

CONTENTS

PREFACE

This is no ordinary rose book as it sweeps away the traditional idea of growing roses on their own and instead shows how effectively roses can be combined with many other ornamental plants in garden design.

Even 'rose purists' are accepting the idea of mixing roses with shrubs, perennials, bulbs, climbers and other ornamentals; and the Royal National Rose Society, at their world-famous gardens in Hertfordshire, are also associating roses with a great many other plants to create greater interest for visitors and to stimulate ideas leading to more adventurous gardening.

In my book I suggest how to combine roses with other plants when designing modern mixed borders, cottage and country gardens, and when planting banks and patio containers.

To create colour on higher levels I have suggested some beautiful combinations of climbing roses and other climbing plants, while for gardeners who want beds of bush roses, I suggest how to ensure colour and interest in these beds all the year round.

Roses have lots of other uses, too: some can be used to create a colourful hedge, as a boundary or garden divider. Others can even be grown in a woodland garden, or allowed to scramble through large trees and conifers. Plenty of examples of good varieties of roses are described throughout the book, and all aspects of rose care are covered in detail.

I hope that the traditional rose bed – nothing but bare twigs for the best part of three seasons – will soon be a thing of the past.

A.T.

1

THE ADAPTABLE ROSE

Whatever part of the garden you are designing, roses can be included for colour and scent in spring, summer and autumn; and even for winter colour if you take into consideration, as you certainly should, the colourful fruits or hips and thorns of many kinds. Many roses have far more to offer than simply flowers. The foliage of some is very attractive for the greater part of the year and with others it takes on colourful autumn tints.

Roses can be mass planted in beds of their own; grown in mixed borders; and even planted in woodland.

They can be grown in ornamental containers on the patio; used as ground cover, particularly on steep and difficult banks; and grown as hedges to provide a boundary around the garden, or to divide the garden if you are creating 'gardens within a garden'.

Roses can provide colour on walls, fences, pergolas and arches. They can be grown up pillars and even into tall mature trees and conifers. Of course, it is a case of choosing suitable kinds for all of these situations, but there is no lack of choice in the vast world of the rose.

From the garden-design point of view roses can be roughly placed into two groups – the old-fashioned varieties and the modern, often highly bred roses. I feel that it is sensible to choose roses to suit the style of garden, although there are certainly no hard and fast rules. I merely put forward the suggestions that old-fashioned, informal roses are a good choice for cottage and old country gardens, and that more formal modern roses look most at home in contemporary gardens.

I feel strongly that roses should not be grown on their own, as they often were in the past. In the late autumn, winter and spring beds of, say, large-flowered (hybrid tea) and cluster-flowered (floribunda) roses simply consist of bare twigs. This was a common sight in many gardens once upon a time, but today most people grow other plants with their roses so that beds and borders provide colour and interest all the year round.

Roses of all kinds should be considered in conjunction with other plants such as shrubs, hardy perennials and bulbs, when planning your planting schemes. But these companion plants must be chosen with care as they should contrast or harmonize with the roses in colour, shape and even in texture.

These ideas form the theme of this book, which is about using roses in the overall design of a garden.

GROWING CONDITIONS

If roses are to grow and flower well they must be given optimum conditions, for although very adaptable they will not grow if soil and aspect are unsuitable.

Aspect and shelter

Roses like plenty of sun so try to choose a spot that receives sun for most of the day, although they will not object if the sun passes off in, say, mid-afternoon. Some roses will grow in dappled shade cast by trees and others will grow and flower well on north-facing walls, but roses will not be happy in permanent heavy shade. Their growth will be weak and spindly and they will produce few if any flowers.

If your garden is very exposed you should try to shelter roses from cold drying winds. Avoid areas where there might be wind funnelling – this can occur in the space between two houses.

There are several ways of providing shelter for roses in exposed gardens: in large gardens a tall windbreak of broad-leaved trees or conifers could be planted on the windward side of the site. The whitebeam, *Sorbus aria,* or the Leyland cypress, × *Cupressocyparis leylandii,* are very suitable. In smaller gardens shelter can be provided with hedges or fences.

Soils

Roses are very adaptable as far as soils are concerned – the essential requirements are high fertility and good drainage (there must be no waterlogging in the winter).

Most soil types found in gardens are suitable, from light sandy kinds to heavy clays. Chalk soils are suitable, too, provided they have sufficient depth of topsoil – at least 30 cm (12 in). This is rarely found in very chalky areas, so it will be advisable to buy in a load of topsoil to increase the depth: ideally up to 45 cm (18 in).

The ideal soil for roses is a fertile medium loam – though you will be lucky if you have this type in your garden. Light and heavy loams are also suitable.

Any soil which stays very wet, or becomes waterlogged, especially in winter, is highly unsuitable, as roses need well-drained conditions. Drainage can be improved by soil cultivation.

It is safe to say that virtually all garden soils will need improving before planting roses – unless you are lucky enough to have a highly fertile medium loam! Details of soil improvement will be found in Chapter 7.

Finally a word about pH – the acidity or alkalinity of the soil. The ideal for roses is a slightly acid soil with a pH of 6–6.5. You can ascertain the state of your soil by testing it with one of the inexpensive proprietary soil-testing kits. I would only advise applying lime (to raise the pH) if your soil is excessively acid – say with a pH of around 4–4.5. Even then only give a very light dressing of lime – a dusting on the soil surface, then working it well into the topsoil.

2

IDEAS FOR MODERN GARDENS

The large-flowered (hybrid tea) and cluster-flowered (floribunda) roses are highly suited to modern gardens (as opposed to old country and cottage gardens) such as those of town houses and houses in cities and urban areas. These gardens can be made highly colourful throughout summer and into autumn with beds of large-flowered and cluster-flowered roses, with perhaps some standard roses, too, to give height to the planting scheme.

It is these kinds – which are classed as 'modern' roses – that I want to concentrate on in this chapter, plus modern repeat-flowering climbing roses (which produce several flushes of blooms in the summer and autumn) and modern roses for hedges.

ROSE BEDS

The large-flowered and cluster-flowered roses are generally grown in their own special beds. Rose purists will not grow any other plants with their beloved flower, but most 'ordinary gardeners', who want colour and interest over as much of the year as possible, will undoubtedly have underplantings of various low-growing plants, especially to provide colour when the roses are at their dullest in late autumn, winter and spring.

Generally these rather formal-looking roses give the best effect in a group of formal beds – beds of regular shapes, such as squares, rectangles and triangles.

A good place for a group of formal beds is alongside a patio or sitting area, near to the house.

However, there is no reason why the beds should not be of irregular shape, if you prefer. The roses will show up really well if the beds are set in a lawn – there is nothing better than a plain green background to set off rose blooms. Alternatively a gravelled or paved area would be suitable as the colourful blooms would then have a rather neutral background.

Why am I suggesting a group of beds rather than just one? This is because I feel the best effect is achieved if only one variety of rose is planted in a bed. With a single bed one tends to plant many varieties in it so the overall effect is spotty. Furthermore the varieties will probably vary in height which does not create a very pleasing picture.

So I am suggesting a group of, say, five beds, with a different variety of rose in each (see Fig. 1). In the centre bed I suggest quite a tall variety. Ideally the roses in the other beds should be somewhat shorter, but all of the same height. A standard rose in each bed will provide further colour on a higher level.

If you have, or only want, one bed and wish to grow several varieties I suggest planting the roses in bold groups as opposed to single bushes, again to avoid a 'spotty' effect. This may mean cutting down on the number of varieties you are able to accommodate, but I can assure you the resultant effect will be well worth it. How do you get over the problem of different heights? Well, you could have the tallest varieties in the centre of the bed and gradually grade down to the edges all round with shorter varieties. By planting in this way none of the roses will be obscured by other bushes (Fig. 2).

By the way, there is no reason why you should not

Shrub roses are excellent subjects for a mixed border and can be combined with perennials like lupins and silver-foliage plants.

Modern rugosa roses are excellent subjects for the modern mixed border and they flower profusely.

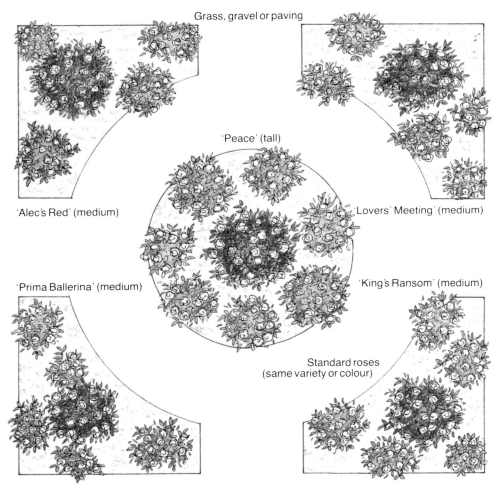

Grass, gravel or paving

'Peace' (tall)

'Alec's Red' (medium)

'Lovers' Meeting' (medium)

'Prima Ballerina' (medium)

'King's Ransom' (medium)

Standard roses
(same variety or colour)

Fig. 1. Formal-looking roses, like the large-flowered varieties, look best in a group of formal beds, with one variety per bed. A standard rose in the middle of each bed gives colour on a higher level.

use both large-flowered and cluster-flowered roses in any planting scheme.

Due consideration should be given to colour planning if you decide to have several varieties in one bed. With one variety per bed there is no risk of colours clashing for the beds are well separated by paths. Fortunately not too many rose colours clash, but I would advise against placing pink varieties next to oranges as this combination gives a rather uneasy effect. To get over this problem you could separate these two colours with white – there are some superb white-flowered roses available today. But most of the other colours go well enough together: reds with yellows and oranges, reds with pinks, and yellows with pinks. Or you may like to try something completely different – a single-colour scheme. How about beds with roses in various shades of red; shades of yellow; pinks; or oranges?

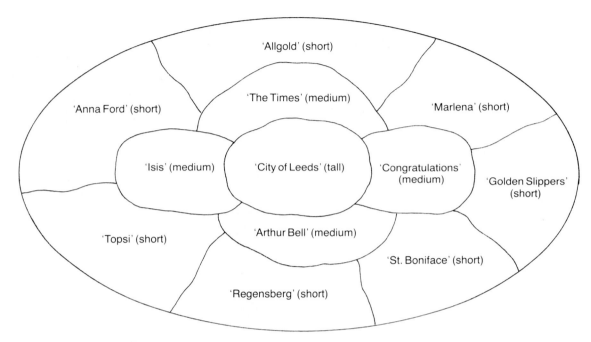

'Allgold' (short)

'Anna Ford' (short)

'The Times' (medium)

'Marlena' (short)

'Isis' (medium)

'City of Leeds' (tall)

'Congratulations' (medium)

'Golden Slippers' (short)

'Topsi' (short)

'Arthur Bell' (medium)

'St. Boniface' (short)

'Regensberg' (short)

Fig. 2. When several varieties of bush roses are to be planted in one bed, set them in bold groups. Have the tallest varieties in the centre and gradually grade down to the edge with shorter varieties. This bed contains a collection of cluster-flowered varieties.

Underplanting roses

As I mentioned earlier, few gardeners will wish to have rose beds which contain only roses, as there will be nothing of interest in the seasons when the roses are but bare twigs. So let us consider some low-growing plants which can be used to plant around the roses, really acting as ground cover, or with which to edge rose beds. Plants chosen should not compete with roses for colour and interest, when the bushes are in flower in the summer. Some of the plants can be summer flowering by all means, but they should have subtle qualities. Blue, purple or mauve flowers go well with roses.

For spring colour there are many miniature bulbs which could be drifted among the bushes or used to edge the beds, like scillas, chionodoxas, muscari, *Crocus chrysanthus* varieties and small bulbous irises.

Spring bedding plants can also be recommended: forget-me-nots would create a blue haze under the bushes if mass planted. Polyanthus, too, are ideal and come in many colours. Winter-flowering pansies, such as the 'Univeral' mixture, bloom throughout winter and into spring. Coming into flower with the roses is London pride, or *Saxifraga × urbium*, with clouds of pale pink flowers and attractive evergreen foliage, making good permanent ground cover.

Also flowering in spring are the perennials aubrieta, with greyish foliage and flowers in shades of purple, blue, pink, red, etc, and the yellow-flowered *Alyssum saxatile*, also with greyish foliage.

Flowering in spring and summer is the lesser periwinkle, *Vinca minor*, an evergreen perennial with blue, purple or white flowers. It makes excellent ground cover, as does *Cerastium tomentosum*, or snow-in-summer, with evergreen silvery foliage and

A beautiful 'cool' scheme, featuring a white climbing rose and perennials with bold fresh green foliage.

'Ballerina' is a small growing, modern repeat–flowering shrub rose whose huge clusters of flowers give a magnificent display over a long period. It combines well with many plants in the modern shrub border.

white flowers. Also with attractive silvery foliage is *Stachys lanata* 'Silver Carpet', an excellent evergreen ground-cover perennial. These two silver-leaved plants make an excellent background for the roses in summer as well as providing winter interest. They are an ideal choice for beds of pink or red roses.

The prostrate perennial *Acaena microphylla* has bronzy green foliage and from early summer onwards produces globular crimson flowers. It is, though, essentially a foliage ground-cover plant.

The ajugas or bugles are excellent evergreen ground-cover perennials grown mainly for their foliage, although they produce flower spikes, usually blue, in spring. Choose *A. reptans* varieties like 'Autropurpurea' with purple foliage; 'Burgundy Glow' with wine-red leaves; or 'Variegata' with cream and green variegated leaves.

The summer flowering ground-cover campanulas or bell flowers have blue flowers and particularly recommended are *C. portenschlagiana* and *C. poscharskyana.*

Geranium 'Johnson's Blue' flowers in summer and goes well with roses, but use it only with the taller-growing varieties as it attains over 30 cm (12 in) in height.

Summer bedding plants such as ageratum, blue lobelia, and pansies and violas, particularly the blue varieties, can also be used to underplant roses, or for edging the beds.

Varieties of the common sage, *Salvia officinalis*, make excellent evergreen ground cover and I recommend 'Icterina' with green and gold foliage; 'Purpurascens' with purple leaves; and 'Tricolor' which is grey-green and white, flushed purple and pink.

Ceratostigma willmottianum is a low ground-cover shrub which produces blue flowers from mid-summer to late autumn. The foliage takes on reddish tints in the autumn.

I suggest all of these plants are mass planted for best effect – in drifts between the rose bushes, or used for edging the beds. Use them as ground-cover plants to cover the soil completely. If you have a group of rose beds a pleasing effect could be obtained by choosing a different type of plant for each bed. For a single bed of roses you could plant several different kinds of plant in bold groups to create a patchwork underplanting.

LARGE-FLOWERED AND CLUSTER-FLOWERED ROSES

These are also known as bush roses because they develop into bushes of quite regular outline. They are very highly bred modern roses and, compared to the old roses and to species, they look rather 'artificial'. But they make a magnificent show of colour during summer and into autumn as they produce several flushes of blooms, starting in early summer. Plant 60 cm (24 in) apart each way.

The large-flowered roses grow, on average, to about 1 m (3 ft) in height but some are taller, up to 1.2 or 1.5 m (4 or 5 ft). There are short ones, too, at around 60 cm (2 ft). They produce large perfectly shaped individual flowers. Some varieties are highly scented, others have virtually no scent. There is a very wide range of colours.

The cluster-flowered roses vary in height from about 45 cm (18 in) to at least 1.8 m (6 ft), but on average they attain 1–1.2 m (3–4 ft), in height. They produce their flowers in clusters and have a slightly less formal appearance than the large-flowered varieties.

Many new varieties of both appear in the rose catalogues each year. Below I have described those I consider some of the best – both older and brand-new varieties.

Large-flowered varieties

'ADOLPH HORSTMANN' Bronze-yellow flowers, slightly scented; medium height.

'ALEC'S RED' Deep red, superb scent; medium height.

'ALEXANDER' Brilliant vermilion; tall grower.

'BLESSINGS' Pinky salmon, well scented; medium height.

'ELIZABETH HARKNESS' Very well scented, creamy blooms flushed with pink; medium height.

'FRAGRANT CLOUD' Tremendous fragrance from the scarlet blooms; medium height.

'GRANDPA DICKSON' Lemon yellow; medium height.

'JUST JOEY' Coppery orange, scented; medium height.

'KING'S RANSOM' One of the best yellows; medium height.

'LOVER'S MEETING' Tangerine orange blooms, slightly fragrant, set against bronze foliage; medium height.

'NATIONAL TRUST' Deep crimson scarlet, not much scent; medium height.

'PAPA MEILLAND' Velvety deep crimson, highly fragrant; medium height.

'PASCALI' Cream-white; medium grower.

'PEACE' Large cream-yellow blooms, flushed pink; tall grower.

'PICCADILLY' Very popular red and gold variety; medium height.

'PRIMA BALLERINA' Rose pink, highly fragrant; medium height.

'SHOWMAN' A newish pure white variety; medium height.

'SILVER JUBILEE' Apricot pink and cream; medium height.

'TROIKA' Bronzy orange, fragrant; medium height.

'WHISKY MAC' Gold and bronze, fragrant; medium height.

Cluster-flowered varieties

'ALLGOLD' Deep yellow; short grower.

'ANNA WHEATCROFT' Light vermilion, slight scent; short grower.

'ARTHUR BELL' Golden yellow, fragrant; medium height.

'BEAUTIFUL BRITAIN' Tomato red flowers; medium grower.

'CIRCUS' Shades of yellow, red, orange and pink; medium grower.

'CITY OF LEEDS' Deep salmon blooms; tall grower.

'CONGRATULATIONS' Large salmon pink blooms on a medium bush.

'ELIZABETH OF GLAMIS' Strongly scented deep salmon blooms; medium height.

'GOLDEN SLIPPERS' Gold flowers from rich orange buds, excellent bedding rose; short grower.

'ICEBERG' Pure white, one of the best in this colour; tall grower.

'ISIS' Well-shaped, fragrant white blooms; medium height.

'KORONA' Glowing orange-red; medium grower.

'KORRESIA' Golden yellow, fragrant; medium height.

'LILI MARLENE' Crimson-scarlet; medium height.

'MASQUERADE' Deep yellow buds, opening to pink, changing to orange then crimson. Huge trusses; tall grower.

'MOUNTBATTEN' Pure yellow blooms; tall grower.

'PICASSO' Pink and white, splashed crimson; medium height.

'PINK PARFAIT' Well-shaped pink flowers on a tall bush.

'SCENTED AIR' Salmon pink, delightfully fragrant flowers on a medium to tall bush.

'THE TIMES' Deep crimson-red, ideal for mass bedding; medium height.

STANDARD ROSES

As I mentioned earlier, standard roses are useful for planting in beds of bush roses to give extra height. Really they are like small trees with a straight stem and a bushy head. Generally they are varieties of large-flowered and cluster-flowered roses budded at a height of about 1 m (3 ft) above ground. However,

Lavender is a marvellous companion plant for roses and here combines beautifully with a group of pink standards.

Lavender, white-flowered perennials and a tree with greeny-gold foliage contrast beautifully with these pink bush roses.

sometimes other kinds of roses, such as shrub roses, are grown as standards.

Then there are weeping standards which have an umbrella-shaped head of long pendulous branches. Varieties of rambler rose are budded on a stem about 1.5 m (5 ft) high.

From the design point of view try to use the same variety of standard as the bush rose below it. Weeping standards could, perhaps, be used as specimens in a lawn.

I am not going to give a list of recommended varieties of large-flowered and cluster-flowered standards as it is a case of looking through the rose catalogues to see what individual growers have to offer. However, you will find many of the varieties I have described above offered as standards.

Shrub-rose standards

Again these vary from one grower to another, but you should find the following listed in catalogues:
'BALLERINA' A very bushy head bearing masses of small pink white-centred flowers over a long period.
'CANARY BIRD' Single bright yellow flowers which appear in the spring.
'NOZOMI' A ground-cover rose often produced as a standard. The small blooms are white touched with pink and it has a semi-weeping head. It has a long flowering season.

Weeping standards

'CRIMSON SHOWER' Beautiful crimson flowers.
'DOROTHY PERKINS' Rose pink.
'FRANÇOIS JURANVILLE' Salmon pink.
'NEW DAWN' Palest pink.

COLOUR ON HIGHER LEVELS

However small a garden may be there is always space – vertical space – for climbing roses to provide colour on higher levels.

Those I want to discuss here, for modern gardens, are the modern repeat-flowering climbers – in other words, those which have several flushes of blooms during summer and autumn. They have a very long season of interest and this is particularly important in small gardens where plants with fleeting beauty are not really worthy of garden space.

Where to grow climbers

A most attractive way of growing climbing roses is on pillars or tripods, either in a border or a specimens in a lawn. A pillar (Fig. 3a) is simply a stout wooden post with at least 2.4 m (8 ft) above ground level and buried 1–1.2 m (3–4 ft) deep in the ground. If this depth seems a bit difficult to achieve, use instead proprietary metal post supports which are easily hammered into the ground. Suitable posts are square fencing posts, at least 8 cm (3 in) square.

If you want a larger feature consider a tripod (Fig. 3b): three posts inserted in triangle formation, leaning inwards and lashed together at the top (rather like a wigwam). Again the height needs to be about 2.4 m (8 ft) above ground level for most climbers. Then plant a rose against each post, preferably using the same variety. When established and flowering well you will have a magnificent pyramid of colour.

Any wall or fence is suitable for roses – sunny walls especially, although there are some climbing roses which will flower well on a shady north-facing wall (see below). The roses can be supported by means of horizontal galvanized wires stretched about 30 cm (12 in) apart and secured with vine eyes, which hold them a little away from the wall. This gap ensures

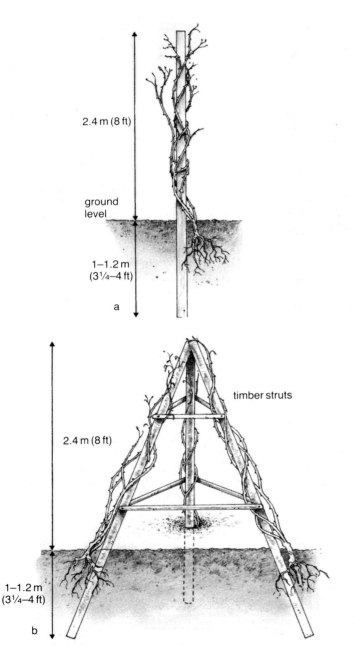

2.4 m (8 ft)

ground
level

1–1.2 m
(3¼–4 ft)

a

2.4 m (8 ft)

timber struts

1–1.2 m
(3¼–4 ft)

b

good air circulation behind the roses, which reduces risk of the fungal disease, rose mildew.

Trellis-work screens about 1.8–2.4 m (6–8 ft) high used to divide a garden make excellent supports for climbing roses. Plant climbers 2.4 m (8 ft) apart on walls, fences and trellis.

Timber pergolas also make excellent supports. Modern-looking ones are available in kit form, or you could perhaps make your own. Particularly attractive are pergolas with brick pillars supporting the top timbers (Fig. 4). Plant a climbing rose at each pillar or post. A pergola can be erected over a patio or path.

An ornamental arch over a gate makes a superb support for a climbing rose; or rather two – plant one at each side of the arch and train them up to meet at the top (Fig. 5).

Companion plants

Of course, climbing roses can be grown on their own, or you may like to combine other climbing plants with them, perhaps allowing them to intertwine.

The climbing hydrangea, *H. petiolaris,* with its greenish white flowers which appear with the first roses of summer, looks superb with a red rose such as 'Dortmund'. This hydrangea will grow well in sun or shade so is suitable for a north-facing wall.

Large-flowered clematis hybrids are undoubtedly the most popular climbing plants and they associate extremely well with roses, particularly blue or purple clematis with red or pink roses. Often recommended are the Jackmanii and Viticella groups of clematis. These bloom in late summer and autumn on current year's shoots and are best pruned hard in late winter each year, to within 30 cm (12 in) of the ground. If not pruned hard they became very bare at the base with all the flowers at the tops of the plants. Recommended varieties are 'Ernest Markham', petunia red; 'Huldine',

Fig. 3. An attractive way of growing climbing roses is to train them up pillars *(a)* and tripods *(b)*. These can be set in a border or used as features in a lawn.

A marvellous contrast in colour and texture. Beds of red floribunda roses boldly edged with catmint or nepeta.

A deep green yew hedge is a traditional backing for a rose bed or garden and the blooms show up really well against it.

pearly white; 'Jackmanii Superba', deep violet-purple; 'Mrs Cholmondeley', pale blue; and 'Perle d'Azure', light blue. Clematis are best with their stems in sun and the roots shaded.

Large-leaved ivies with deep green glossy foliage are a marvellous foil for yellow or white roses. Being evergreen they have year-round interest and can be grown in sun or shade. Ivies which fit the bill include *Hedera canariensis*, the Canary Island ivy; and *H. colchica*, the Persian ivy. Both are vigorous but easily controlled by pruning in spring.

Blue-flowered climbers combine well with red or pink roses. *Solanum crispum* 'Glasnevin' has purple-blue flowers like its relative the potato, and blooms

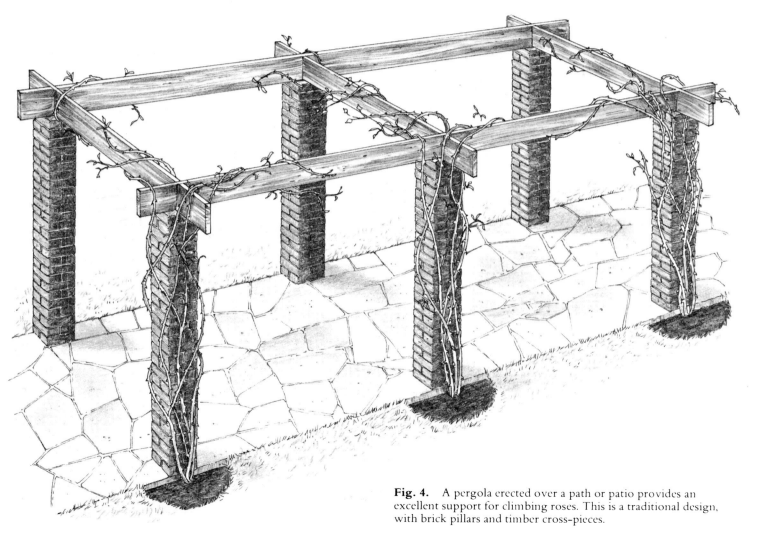

Fig. 4. A pergola erected over a path or patio provides an excellent support for climbing roses. This is a traditional design, with brick pillars and timber cross-pieces.

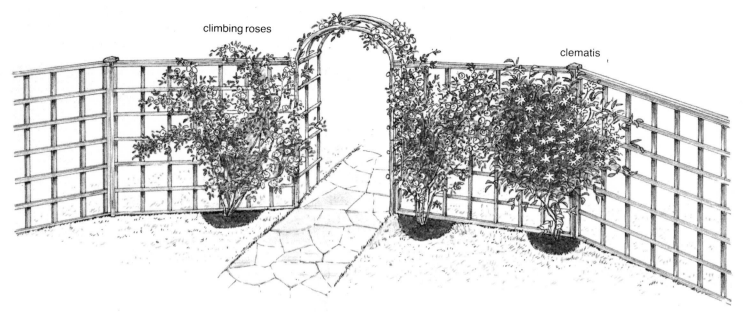

climbing roses

clematis

Fig. 5. An ornamental arch and trellis screens clothed with climbing roses and clematis. Plant a rose at each side of an arch and train them up to meet at the top.

in summer and autumn. It needs a sunny position. *Wisteria floribunda* 'Macrobotrys' has lilac flowers, tinged with bluish purple, in late spring/early summer, and also needs plenty of sun.

Modern repeat-flowering climbers

These produce several flushes of blooms during summer and autumn. The flowers are often large – sometimes resembling those of hybrid teas, sometimes those of floribundas.

'ALOHA' Suitable for a north wall. Large coral pink double flowers; height 2.4 m (8 ft).

'ALTISSIMO' Large single velvety red flowers; height up to 4.5 m (15 ft).

'BANTRY BAY' Rose pink; height up to 3.6 m (12 ft).

'COMPASSION' Hybrid tea type flowers in salmon, shaded orange, and very fragrant; height 3 m (10 ft).

'DANSE DU FEU' Suitable for a north wall, brilliant orange-red blooms; height 3 m (10 ft).

'DORTMUND' Suitable for a north wall, single flowers, red with a white centre, carried in large clusters; height up to 3.6 m (12 ft).

'GOLDEN SHOWERS' Deservedly popular; suitable for a north wall, large bright yellow blooms; height 2.4 m (8 ft).

'HANDEL' Shapely flowers in cream-white flushed with pink; height about 3 m (10 ft).

'JOSEPH'S COAT' Yellowish orange and red flowers; height up to 2.4 m (8 ft).

'LEVERKUSEN' Double pale yellow flowers; height up to 3 m (10 ft).

'MAIGOLD' Semi-double golden yellow blooms, suitable for north wall; height up to 3 m (10 ft).

'NEW DAWN' Suitable for growing on a north wall. Palest pink blooms, moderate vigour; reaching a height of about 1.8 m (6 ft).

'PARKDIREKTOR RIGGERS' Single bright scarlet flowers; height about 2.4 m (8 ft).

'PINK PERPÉTUÉ' Bright pink flowers in large clusters; height about 2.4 m (8 ft).

'SCHOOLGIRL' Large coppery apricot blooms flushed with pink. Hybrid-tea shaped and fragrant; height 3 m (10 ft).

'SWAN LAKE' White with pink tinge. Hybrid-tea shaped blooms; height about 2.4 m (8 ft).

'SYMPATHIE' Hybrid-tea shaped flowers in bright scarlet; suitable for north wall and growing to at least 3 m (10 ft) in height.

MODERN ROSES FOR HEDGES

A rose hedge makes an interesting feature in modern gardens, whether as a boundary or as a garden divider. There are a great many modern roses which can be used for hedging but those which I consider are among the very best for the purpose are listed below.

If you want a low hedge, under 1.2 m (4 ft) in height, allow about 45 cm (18 in) between each rose. I can recommend the shrub rose 'Ballerina', which is repeat flowering. It is described in Chapter 4.

For taller hedges, 1.2–2.4 m (4–8 ft) in height you will need to plant 1 m (3 ft) apart. The following, all of which I recommend, are also covered in more detail in Chapter 4: 'Chinatown' (repeat-flowering shrub rose); 'Felicia' (hybrid musk); 'Hunter' (a *rugosa* variety); 'Kordes' Robusta' (a *rugosa* variety); 'Marguerite Hilling' (repeat-flowering shrub rose); 'Nevada' (repeat-flowering shrub rose); and 'Penelope' (a hybrid musk).

I can also recommend for a tall hedge 'Queen Elizabeth', a very popular cluster-flowered rose with bright pink flowers. It will grow to 3 m (10 ft) in height but can be cut back about 1 m (3 ft) below the height you require. There is also a brilliant orange-scarlet form of this widely planted rose, 'Scarlet Queen Elizabeth'.

3

PATIOS AND CONTAINERS

Growing plants in ornamental containers on patios, balconies and roof gardens has never been more popular than it is today. The most widely used plants for providing colour are spring and summer bedding plants, and spring bulbs, but gardeners are beginning to realize that there are many more types of plants that are suited to container growing, especially various permanent kinds, including roses.

The main groups of roses for containers are the miniatures, the small-growing cluster-flowered or floribundas, which many rose catalogues now list as patio roses, and the low-growing polyantha roses. Small climbers can be used, too, if you want to provide colour on a wall.

All these roses can be effectively used in small beds around or on the patio, perhaps with other plants to provide colour when the roses are out of flower.

Furthermore, all of these groups of roses are the ideal choices for general planting in very small gardens – for example, in the typical pocket-handkerchief gardens of modern town houses.

TYPES OF CONTAINER

Various kinds of containers can be used for roses, but do bear in mind minimum depths: these are 22 cm (9 in) for miniature roses and 38 cm (15 in) for small cluster-flowered, polyantha roses and small climbers. These minimum depths will give the plants adequate root run but can be increased with advantage. For instance, 30 × 30 cm (12 × 12 in) tubs are useful for miniatures; and 45 × 45 cm (18 × 18 in) or larger for others.

John Innes potting compost

layer of roughage

5 cm (2 in) layer drainage material

Fig. 6. A large wooden tub in traditional style – an excellent container for roses. All containers should have drainage material in the bottom, and can be filled with John Innes potting compost.

The style of container should, of course, match the surroundings. For instance, a patio in a cottage or country garden calls for wooden tubs, perhaps cut-down wooden barrels. Fig. 6 shows a traditional wooden tub. Terracotta or stone tubs would also be in keeping.

In a modern setting choose from contemporary styles of timber, concrete or reconstituted-stone tubs.

Window boxes are suitable containers for miniature roses but again do make sure they are sufficiently deep. The absolute minimum dimensions for a box are 25 cm (10 in) deep and 25 cm wide. Traditional wooden boxes are recommended, or you may prefer one in terracotta clay, which is particularly in keeping in a country- or cottage-garden setting.

All of these materials are porous, that is, they allow air to enter through the sides. This is needed by roses, so avoid non-porous tubs such as those made from plastic.

All containers must have drainage holes in the bottom and are best supported slightly above ground level on small blocks of wood or bits of broken paving slabs. This allows surplus water to quickly drain away and so prevents waterlogging.

PREPARING AND PLANTING CONTAINERS

When each container is in position place in the bottom a 5 cm (2 in) layer of drainage material such as broken clay flower pots, stones or pebbles and top this with a thin layer of rough peat or leafmould. Fill with soil-based compost, such as John Innes potting compost No. 2 or 3.

The number of roses you will be able to plant in each container depends of course on its size: miniature roses need to be spaced 30 cm (12 in) apart each way; small cluster-flowered roses 45 cm (18 in) apart each way;

and allow 45–60 cm (18–24 in) each way for polyantha roses. So there may be room only for one rose per container – never pack them in close together. Climbers should certainly be planted one per container.

COMPANION PLANTS

Provided space allows, suitable companion plants could be planted around the edge of containers to provide colour when the roses are out of flower. Miniature spring-flowering bulbs are a good choice, including the blue-flowered grape hyacinths (*Muscari*), glory of the snow (*Chionodoxa*) and scillas. Snowdrops (*Galanthus*) will flower in winter and so too will the yellow winter aconites (*Eranthis*).

Purple-leaved or variegated bugles or ajugas will trail over the edge and produce blue flowers in the spring. If you want extra colour in the summer use trailing bedding plants around the edge, like blue or multicoloured lobelia or blue violas.

If the roses are grown in beds then you can combine with them not only miniature bulbs and the other plants recommended above, but also some small compact shrubs, particularly those which will act as a foil to the bright colours of the roses. Grey foliage combines well with roses, such as that of the cotton lavender, *Santolina chamaecyparissus corsica* (also known as 'Nana') with silvery, woolly finely cut foliage; and the dwarf lavender, *Lavandula angustifolia* 'Hidcote', with grey-green leaves and spikes of violet flowers in summer.

Foliage perennials of carpeting habit could also be drifted among the roses, like *Stachys lanata* 'Silver Carpet', with its silver-grey woolly leaves. I have seen evergreen bergenias used effectively among miniature and small-growing roses, with their bold leathery leaves and pink, red or white flowers in late winter and early spring.

The more restrained ground-cover ivies also make a good foil when drifted among the bushes, or allowed to trail over the edges of small beds. Try such varieties as 'Adam', 'Caenwoodiana', 'Deltoidea', 'Green Ripple', 'Manda's Crested' and 'Très Coup'. All of these are varieties of the common ivy, *Hedera helix*.

Prostrate junipers make good foliage companions for miniature and small-growing roses. These include the *Juniperus horizontalis* varieties 'Bar Harbor' with grey-blue foliage; 'Glauca', steel-blue; 'Emerald Spreader', emerald green; and 'Turquoise Spreader', turquoise green.

RECOMMENDED VARIETIES

Miniature roses

These are the smallest roses available and attain no more than 45 cm (18 in) in height. They flower profusely throughout summer, bearing tiny blooms like scaled-down versions of large-flowered and cluster-flowered roses. They are extremely popular in America and are at last being used much more in Britain.

As well as being suitable for containers and small beds, a collection of them will create a pleasing feature in a raised bed, say alongside a patio.

Rose catalogues now list many varieties so I have picked out those which I consider are the very best.
'ANGELA RIPPON' No more than 30 cm (12 in) in height, this popular variety has double flowers in a beautiful shade of salmon.
'BABY GOLDSTAR' Hybrid-tea shaped blooms in a superb shade of golden yellow, carried on 22 cm (9 in) high plants.
'BABY MASQUERADE' This has been around for some years and has never lost its popularity. The yellow, pink and red flowers are produced throughout summer.
'BENSON AND HEDGES SPECIAL' The golden blooms, larger than most, are produced throughout the season.
'COLIBRI' A popular variety with double flowers in golden orange, heavily flushed with red.

'CORALIN' This one has bright orange-red flowers and creates a real impact if planted in a bold group.
'DARLING FLAME' Another eye-catcher, in bright orange-scarlet. It's a new variety which is bound to become popular.
'GENTLE TOUCH' This was voted Rose of the Year in 1986. It has pale pink blooms like small-scale hybrid teas and they are carried in large clusters, creating a profusion of colour. Height is 45 cm (18 in). It's also listed as a patio rose.
'MAGIC CAROUSEL' This delightful little variety is basically white but the edges of the petals are shaded with carmine-red.
'PERLE D'ALCANADA' Bushy plant with deep crimson blooms.
'POUR TOI' One of the great miniature roses – white, flushed with cream at the base of the petals.
'ROSINA' Miniature hybrid-tea-like flowers in bright yellow, produced throughout summer.
'ROYAL SALUTE' Very bushy little plant bearing scented rose pink blooms.
'SNOWBALL' This has very tiny rounded blooms in pure white – new, and bound to become very popular.
'SWEET FAIRY' Well-scented miniature with lilac-pink flowers.

Low-growing cluster-flowered varieties

These are also known as dwarf floribundas, and some catalogues are listing them as patio roses. They grow to no more than 45 cm (18 in) in height and are ideal for containers or small beds and borders. They produce clusters of small flowers with great freedom.
'ANNA FORD' This has a bushy spreading habit of growth and bears in great profusion mandarin-red flowers, which turn to orange-red as they age.
'BRIGHT SMILE' This is a comparatively new variety with bright yellow flowers carried in large clusters.
'KERRY GOLD' The shiny deep green foliage is a perfect background for the deep golden flowers.

Clematis of all kinds are attractive companions for roses. Here a clematis is being grown up a pillar in a bed of shrub roses.

This is a daring colour scheme but it works: cerise verbena and vermilion bush roses. This scheme is guaranteed to attract attention.

'MARLENA' Popular variety which produces masses of brilliant, glowing crimson blooms.

'REGENSBERG' This is a comparatively new variety which has double pink and white flowers.

'ST BONIFACE' Another fairly new variety with brilliant vermilion, well-shaped flowers.

'TOPSI' Plant this in a bold group for a really stunning display. The blooms are brilliant orange-scarlet.

Polyantha roses

These are low-growing shrub roses, varying in height from 30 to 90 cm (12 to 36 in), and producing clusters of small blooms through summer and into autumn. Suitable for large containers as well as for small beds and borders.

'BABY FAURAX' An old variety, 22 cm (9 in) tall, with unusual pale violet flowers.

'ELLEN POULSEN' One of the best polyantha roses, with rose pink flowers in profusion; height about 60 cm (24 in).

'LITTLE WHITE PET' A short grower – 45 cm (18 in) – with masses of tiny double white blooms produced with great freedom. An old variety but still one of the best.

'PAUL CRAMPEL' Bushy, free-flowering variety with orange-scarlet blooms.

'THE FAIRY' A bushy plant 45 cm (18 in) high with dainty sprays of rose pink flowers from mid-summer to late autumn.

'YVONNE RABIER' An old variety, bushy and attaining about 45 cm (18 in) in height, with small double pure white flowers.

Small-growing climbers

There are several small climbing roses which can be planted singly in tubs, or in small borders. The very vigorous kinds have a more extensive root system and should therefore be avoided for container work.

'ALOHA' This restrained grower gains a height of not more than 2.4 m (8 ft). It's a modern repeat-flowering climber bearing large double salmon pink flowers of hybrid-tea shape.

'COPENHAGEN' Excellent choice for a restrained deep scarlet variety. It has medium-sized hybrid-tea-type flowers and grows about 2.1 m (7 ft) tall.

'GOLDEN SHOWERS' Of similar height to 'Copenhagen', this highly popular climbing rose is repeat-flowering, carrying large, flat, bright yellow blooms against a backcloth of healthy deep green foliage. It has some scent.

'POM-PON DE PARIS' This is an old China rose (introduced 1839), really the only miniature climbing rose. It grows no more than 1.8 m (6 ft) in height and bears tiny leaves and mini but well-shaped pink flowers. It blooms only once in the summer.

4

MIXED BORDERS

Rarely these days do private gardens feature borders of one type of plant (such as a shrub, herbaceous or annual border), but rather the borders in modern gardens are mixed. That is, they contain all kinds of plants – shrubs, roses, hardy perennials, bulbs, annuals and so on.

The main framework of a mixed border generally consists of shrubs – and roses can be included here – and between and around the shrubs are planted other groups of plants. Some of the shrubs should be evergreen – not more than about one-third, though, or a heavy sombre appearance could be the result. The remaining two-thirds would be deciduous shrubs, including roses.

Not all roses by any means look at home in the modern mixed border; the very formal large-flowered and cluster-flowered roses do not fit in too well. I have described ways of using these in Chapter 2. Better suited to the mixed border are the modern shrub roses (both repeat and summer-flowering), the hybrid musk shrub roses, modern varieties of *rugosa* and, of course, the species or wild roses, which are essentially shrubs.

These are the groups of roses I will recommend and describe in this chapter. Their spacing should roughly equal their ultimate height.

COMPANION PLANTS FOR ROSES

When planning a mixed border it is important to group plants pleasingly and not just to plant at random or wherever there is space. When considering roses think carefully about which other plants would look well with them. Consider flower and foliage colour and shape and texture. It is easiest if you plan according to seasons. Try creating, for instance, a group of plants which provide summer colour, a group which will be of interest in winter or spring, and a group for autumn. Let's take a closer look at grouping plants with roses, according to seasons.

A group for summer colour

Most of the roses described later flower in summer and there are plenty of shrubs and perennials which associate particularly well with them. The main colours in roses are shades of red, pink and orange. We may also have some yellow varieties and a few whites. Therefore I consider suitable flower and foliage colours of the shrubs and perennials to be blue, purple, white and silver.

Purple-leaved shrubs look particularly attractive with red or pink roses and one of the best is the purple smoke bush, *Cotinus coggygria* 'Foliis Purpureis' with rich plum-purple leaves. 'Royal Purple' has even deeper wine-purple leaves. Or you may prefer a purple barberry, such as *Berberis* × *ottawensis* 'Purpurea', a vigorous tall shrub with rich purple foliage, far better then the ubiquitous *B. thunbergii atropurpurea*. If you have room for a large tree in the border then consider the purple Norway maple, *Acer platanoides* 'Crimson King' with large hand-shaped leaves of a deep crimson-purple.

Silver or grey foliage shrubs suitable for grouping

Many roses have notable features other than flowers, such as colourful heps (hips) in the autumn. These well deserve a place in the shrub border, combining them with autumn-flowering perennials.

This mellow brick wall is an excellent background for the modern climber 'Iceberg'. The bush roses in front harmonize with the wall.

with shrub and species roses include lavender, like *Lavandula angustifolia* 'Grappenhall'; *Artemisia arborescens,* a small rounded shrub with finely cut silvery foliage; and the weeping silver-leaved pear, *Pyrus salicifolia* 'Pendula', which makes a small tree.

White-flowered shrubs look lovely with red or pink roses and I can particularly recommend the small shrubby cinquefoil, *Potentilla dahurica* 'Farrer's White', or the dwarf grey-leaved 'Manchu'. *Potentilla* 'Vilmoriniana' is a good choice, too, with cream flowers and silvery leaves, making a medium-sized shrub. The mock orange or philadelphus flowers in early summer: there are many to choose from like the large-growing 'Virginal' or the dwarf 'Manteau d'Hermine'.

Blue-flowered shrubs which make good companions for roses of all colours include the ceanothus, like the evergreen 'Burkwoodii' and the deciduous 'Gloire de Versailles'. Both are medium-sized shrubs. *Perovskia atriplicifolia* 'Blue Spire' has grey-green foliage and panicles of lavender blue flowers in late summer. It's a small shrub, as is *Caryopteris × clandonensis* 'Heavenly Blue' with deep blue flowers in late summer. The large-growing *Buddleia alternifolia* makes a superb background for roses, with its scented lilac flowers which appear with the first flush of roses. Shrubby veronicas or hebes make good companions for roses, too. There are lots to choose from, but those with blue flowers include *Hebe × franciscana* 'Blue Gem', a small shrub, and of similar stature 'Midsummer Beauty' with long spikes of lavender blooms.

There are one or two perennials with silvery foliage which I like to include with roses and one is the globe artichoke, *Cynara scolymus,* with grey deeply cut leaves. *C. cardunculus,* the cardoon, has even more striking silvery grey foliage. The Scotch thistle, *Onopordon acanthium,* is a biennial but freely self-sows itself so you will never be without plants. When in flower it towers to at least 1.8 m (6 ft) and has very prickly whitish grey foliage. A marvellous contrast for roses in colour, texture and form if you can find space for it.

Many of the ornamental grasses contrast well with roses. There is the very vigorous gardener's garters, *Phalaris arundinacea* 'Picta', with green and white striped leaves; the grey *Helictotrichon sempervirens;* the dwarf blue-grey *Festuca glauca;* and the yellow-banded *Miscanthus sinensis* 'Zebrinus'.

A dramatic contrast can be provided, too, with *Acanthus mollis latifolius,* which has deeply divided green leaves and spikes of purple and white flowers in summer. Try it with a purple-leaved cotinus and pink or red roses. *Acanthus spinosus* is similar. The same dramatic effect can be achieved with *Eryngium tripartitum,* which has large heads of small steel-blue globular flowers from mid-summer until well into autumn.

Not quite so spectacular, but useful blue-flowered perennials which look lovely grouped around roses include *Campanula lactiflora* 'Pritchard's Variety', *Tradescantia virginiana* varieties which bloom in late summer, and *Salvia superba* with spikes of violet flowers. Try the varieties 'Lubeca' or 'East Friesland'.

Maintaining winter and spring interest

Roses, of course, will not be in flower during these seasons, but try to maintain interest and colour around them, rather than having a dull area in the border. Do not forget that *Rosa omeiensis pteracantha* could be included in a winter/spring group, for its spectacular large red thorns. I like to group around shrub roses varieties of *Helleborus orientalis* or Lenten roses, which flower in late winter and early spring. They send up stems 45 cm (18 in) high carrying bowl-shaped flowers in various colours: white, purple, crimson, pink, red and cream. Some are attractively spotted. Foliage is evergreen. Group with the hellebores some snow-drops, and the winter-flowering iris, *Iris unguicularis,* with pale blue flowers produced intermittently throughout winter. There are all kinds of spring-flowering bulbs that could be planted around the bases of roses or drifted between them, like scillas, chionodoxas, muscari, crocuses, *Tulipa greigii* and *T. kaufmanniana* hybrids and miniature bulbous irises.

Mellow fruitfulness

Many roses are still flowering in the autumn, but equally spectacular will be the hips of certain roses such as *Rosa farreri persetosa*, *R. moyesii* and its variety 'Geranium', *R. pomifera*, *R. eglanteria* and *R. rubrifolia*.

To combine with the autumn rose display we can use shrubs noted for autumn leaf colour and berries, and autumn-flowering perennials.

As a fiery backcloth for the roses try *Cotinus coggygria* 'Flame' whose foliage turns brilliant orange. Plant a pampas grass, too, *Cortaderia selloana* 'Sunningdale Silver' with plumes of white flowers 2.4 m (8 ft) high. Complete the picture by planting at the front of the group some Michaelmas daisies with purple, red or blue flowers, and drift among the plants some autumn crocuses like the lilac blue *C. speciosus*, and some colchicums such as *C. speciosum* and its varieties. I guarantee you will not be disappointed with this group!

If you want to include some autumn-berrying shrubs then consider *Viburnum opulus* 'Compactum', a small shrub with red translucent berries and good autumn foliage colour; *Euonymus europaeus* 'Red Cascade', a medium-sized shrub with red and orange fruits; and *Cotoneaster bullatus floribundus*, a medium-sized shrub weighed down in autumn with red berries. Or you might prefer the yellow-berried *Cotoneaster* 'Rothschildianus', a large bush.

Perennials for autumn include the sedums or stonecrops, like *S. spectabile* 'Autumn Joy' with salmon pink flowers and 'Ruby Glow' in brilliant rose red. The mat-forming polygonums are flowering well into autumn, like *P. vacciniifolium* with spikes of rose pink flowers, and *P. affine* varieties such as 'Darjeeling Red' and the rose-coloured 'Donald Lowndes'. The polygonums can be planted in ground-covering drifts between the roses and in front of them.

ROSES FOR THE MIXED BORDER

Modern repeat-flowering shrub roses

These, in my opinion, are the first choice for a mixed border if you want plenty of colour throughout summer and into autumn. They produce several flushes of blooms throughout the season – hence the term 'repeat-flowering'. Most form quite large bushes and, depending on variety, grow to between 1.5 and 2.4 m (5 and 8 ft) in height. Their spread is usually roughly equal to eventual height, so bear this in mind when planting.

'BALLERINA' One of the smaller modern shrub roses at only about 1.2 m (4 ft) in height. The pink, white-eyed flowers are only small but are carried in huge clusters, giving a magnificent display.

'CARDINAL HUME' A new rose with deep purple fragrant flowers on a low bushy plant.

'CHINATOWN' A vigorous and well-known rose with deep yellow blooms. It will reach a height of about 1.5–1.8 m (5–6 ft).

'ELMSHORN' A medium grower, bushy with large clusters of small, strong pink, double blooms.

'FRED LOADS' A tall variety for the back of the border, bearing large single blooms in vivid orange-vermilion. A real eye-catcher and highly popular.

'GOLDEN WINGS' This tall vigorous variety produces its large, single, scented, light golden yellow flowers against a backcloth of light green foliage. The stamens are an added feature, being quite prominent and amber in colour.

'JOSEPH'S COAT' This is a vigorous tall shrub for the back of the border, with a profusion of semi-double multi-coloured flowers in shades of yellow and red. An outstanding shrub rose in every way.

'KASSEL' Of medium height and very free flowering, this variety has big clusters of double flowers in deep orange-red set against deep green foliage.

A mixed border in late summer, with roses mingling with blue and white hydrangeas.

Purple violas make a stunning underplanting for these pink bush roses.

'LAVENDER LASSIE' A modest grower at about 1.2 m (4 ft) in height, this is especially recommended for its fragrance. The blooms are lavender-pink and carried in big clusters.

'MARGUERITE HILLING' A tall variety at 2.4 m (8 ft) in height, this is a sport of 'Nevada' (see below), bearing palest pink blooms freely.

'NEVADA' An excellent and popular shrub rose up to 2.4 m (8 ft) in height, bearing big single blooms in white, touched with pink on the reverse. It produces one main flush of blooms and a few more later in the season. The almost single blooms have prominent golden stamens.

'WESTERLAND' This is a tall vigorous rose with big clusters of semi-double flowers in brilliant golden orange.

Modern summer-flowering shrub roses

These have one flush of blooms in the summer and then no more until next year. However, while they are in bloom they make a fine display; and remember that they will provide masses of colour over many weeks.

'CONSTANCE SPRY' A vigorous variety at least 2.4 m (8 ft) in height, bearing in early summer sprays of big pink, highly fragrant flowers in profusion. The stems may need some support.

'FRITZ NOBIS' Attaining about 1.8 m (6 ft) in height, this one has semi-double highly scented pale salmon pink blooms in summer, followed by masses of hips.

'FRÜHLINGSGOLD' Up to 2.4 m (8 ft) in height, this is a very popular shrub rose and truly spectacular when in flower. The blooms appear in early summer; they are large, almost single, creamy yellow and fragrant.

'FRÜHLINGSMORGEN' Companion for 'Frühlings-gold', up to 1.8 m (6 ft) in height, this one has large single blooms in deep pink, and eyecatching reddish purple stamens. You may get a few more blooms later in the season.

Hybrid musk roses

This group of shrub roses was evolved in the early part of the twentieth century and is noted for superb scent. The varieties are free-flowering and trouble-free, making them highly popular subjects for the mixed border. Flowers are often produced well into the autumn. Average height is about 1.5 m (5 ft).

'BUFF BEAUTY' This variety has orangy buff-yellow blooms with a superb fragrance, set against attractive bronze-green leaves.

'CORNELIA' This one has small flowers in large sprays, pink with an apricot flush and very highly scented.

'FELICIA' This has the palest pink blooms from bright pink buds, and they are strongly scented. It has a spreading, arching habit of growth.

'MOONLIGHT' The highly scented semi-double blooms are pale cream-white with prominent golden stamens, set against a background of deep green foliage.

'PENELOPE' Semi-double light salmon pink blooms carried in large clusters. A fine and deservedly popular variety.

'PROSPERITY' The well-scented double flowers, pure white, are set against shiny foliage.

Modern rugosas

Rosa rugosa has produced many hybrids, some of which have been introduced in recent years. Those which have single blooms produce good crops of hips in the autumn. The stems are very prickly.

'HUNTER' This is a tall shrub of bushy habit, carrying double bright crimson flowers in summer and repeating in the autumn.

'KORDES' ROBUSTA' This is one of the newest, being introduced in 1982. It reaches about 1.5 m (5 ft) in height and has single brilliant scarlet flowers set against bright green leaves. It flowers very freely throughout the summer.

Species

These are the wild roses, although I have included a few garden varieties. The latter, though, are not highly bred and very much resemble true species. The wild roses may be noted not only for attractive flowers but also for decorative autumn hips or fruits, distinctive foliage or attractive thorns. They are shrubs in every sense of the word and so very much at home in the mixed border with other ornamental shrubs and perennials as companions. The abbreviation *R.* in the following list stands for *Rosa,* the generic name of the rose.

R. cantabrigiensis   A shrub of about 1.5 m (5 ft) in height and spread, bearing light yellow flowers early in the summer which are set against abundant small leaves.

R. ecae 'HELEN KNIGHT'   This modern variety which has small golden yellow flowers, is similar to the species but larger. It has small deep green leaves and ideally should be given some means of support such as a post. If the border is backed by a wall or fence the rose could be effectively trained to this.

R. eglanteria   This is the common sweet briar, which makes a shrub up to about 1.8 m (6 ft) in height. The small light pink blooms are carried singly during the summer. The foliage is apple scented and this is particularly pronounced after a shower of rain. Heavy crops of hips are produced in the autumn.

R. farreri persetosa   Popularly known as the threepenny bit rose. It makes a bush about 1.5 m (5 ft) in height, of rather sprawling habit, and in summer produces lilac-pink blooms. These are followed in autumn by masses of bright orange-red hips. The fine ferny foliage turns to shades of crimson and purple in the autumn.

R. foetida   This is the Austrian briar rose, with single deep yellow flowers in summer. It is a vigorous plant, up to 1.5 m (5 ft) in height, with shiny foliage.

R. gallica complicata   A shrub growing to about 1.5 m (5 ft) in height, but with an arching habit, giving it a spread of up to 2.4 m (8 ft). The big single blooms are pink and produced in midsummer.

R. gallica officinalis   Perhaps better known as the apothecary's rose, the red rose of Lancaster, or the old red damask. The semi-double crimson blooms appear in early summer. It makes a specimen about 1 m (3 ft) in height and spread.

R. moyesii   One of the best roses for autumn hips, which are flagon-shaped and bright waxy red. The single deep red flowers are attractive, too, being produced in summer. All this combined with attractive foliage. There is a well-known variety of this species named 'Geranium', with brilliant red flowers and masses of eye-catching orange-red hips. Both grow to about 2.4 m (8 ft) in height.

R. omeiensis pteracantha   A rose with many attractive features: ferny foliage, large vicious red thorns, which are translucent when young, small single white flowers, and red hips. The flowers are produced in the spring. Ultimate height is about 2.4 m (8 ft) or a little more.

R. pomifera   This is known as the apple rose, presumably because of the large apple-shaped crimson hips which are a feature in the autumn. The single pink summer flowers are set off by attractive bluish green foliage. A vigorous grower at around 1.8 m (6 ft) in height.

R. primula   The incense rose, one of the earliest to bloom. The single small yellow flowers appear in spring and are carried on arching branches. The leaves smell of incense, hence the popular name. Height is around 1.8 m (6 ft).

R. rubrifolia   A modest grower at around 1.2–1.5 m (4–5 ft) in height. This species is noted for its purple-grey foliage carried on deep red stems. The pink flowers are not very showy, but the crops of brown-red autumn hips certainly are. This rose looks lovely planted with a purple cotinus.

R. spinosissima   This is also known as *R. pimpinellifolia,* and popularly as the Scotch or burnet rose. In summer it produces profusion of single cream-white flowers and in autumn crops of almost black hips. It attains about 1.2 m (4 ft) in height.

An unusual combination of red bush roses and yellow Spanish broom, *Spartium junceum*.

The white climbing rose 'Seagull' creates a veritable avalanche of blooms over this pergola.

R. xanthina 'CANARY BIRD' In late spring and early summer this popular rose produces abundant, single, golden yellow flowers. To complement the flowers it has bright green ferny foliage. It is a fairly modest grower, attaining a height of 1.5–1.8 m (5–6 ft).

ROSES FOR WOODLAND PLANTING

Some species roses are suitable for planting in woodland for they will flower well in dappled shade and, even more importantly, they look at home among trees, especially in an 'exotic' woodland – one containing such shrubs as rhododendrons, azaleas, camellias, pieris, magnolias, kalmias, etc. It is best not to subject roses to complete and heavy shade: if these conditions exist in a woodland it would be better to plant the roses at the edge so that they receive some sun. As mentioned above, light dappled shade is perfectly acceptable. The roses which I can recommend for woodland planting have all been described under species. Try the following: *R. eglanteria, R. farreri persetosa, R. moyesii, R. omeiensis pteracantha, R. rubrifolia, R. spinosissima* and *R. xanthina* 'Canary Bird'. In my opinion this last one is the absolute best for woodland as it looks really superb in such a setting.

Of course, there is no reason why climbers and ramblers should not be planted on the edge of woodland, provided they receive sufficient sunshine. For suitable kinds see Chapter 5.

5

COTTAGE AND COUNTRY GARDENS

Rural and semi-rural cottage gardens, and other gardens in the country, are generally very informal with a glorious mixture of colourful plants of all kinds.

Plants which give an old-fashioned atmosphere are invariably chosen for cottage gardens, and often for other country gardens, too. Old-fashioned shrubs and perennials, and certainly roses, are very much part of these gardens. I have therefore devoted this chapter to the old-fashioned roses, and suggest some traditional cottage-garden shrubs and perennials to grow with them.

Traditionally in cottage gardens all kinds of plants are grown together in the beds and borders – shrubs, perennials, roses, hardy annuals, climbers and even vegetables and fruit bushes. An apparently haphazard mixture, but in reality this is not the case, for intensive planting of this kind has to be planned if it is to be kept under control.

It is sensible to group together plants which contrast or harmonize in colour, texture and shape and to ensure that very vigorous plants are not placed next to those of more restrained habit which could then be quickly smothered.

COMPANION PLANTS FOR ROSES

The old-fashioned roses bloom in the summer and therefore the plants that are grouped with them should also be providing colour and interest at this time, contrasting or harmonizing with the roses.

Traditionally country cottages have roses around the front door and very often used for this purpose is the rambler rose 'Paul's Scarlet' with masses of semi-double scarlet-red blooms in summer. Other summer-flowering climbers could be grown with it and what better than some old-fashioned kinds with highly scented flowers, like the white summer jasmine, *Jasminum officinale,* or varieties of honeysuckle, *Lonicera periclymenum.* Although not scented, clematis make lovely companions for 'Paul's Scarlet' and other old-fashioned climbers and ramblers. There are few better than *Clematis* 'Jackmanii Superba' with big deep violet-purple flowers from mid-summer to early autumn. You can let roses and other climbers intertwine but this can make rose pruning a bit difficult. The alternative is to plant side by side but train them apart.

There are lots of old-fashioned shrubs to complement old roses. A particularly lovely combination is the China rose 'Cécile Brunner' with lavender or rue. This rose has small flesh-pink flowers in early and mid-summer and these contrast beautifully with the grey foliage and violet flowers of *Lavandula angustifolia* 'Hidcote' or with the grey-blue foliage of *Ruta graveolens* 'Jackman's Blue'. Both the lavender and rue can, in fact, be effectively planted with any of the old-fashioned roses, especially those with pink or red flowers.

Or try rosemary, *Rosmarinus officinalis,* with pink or red roses, such as the popular old *rugusa,* 'Frau Dagmar Hastrup', which has single clear pink flowers in early summer. The evergreen rosemary has deep green aromatic foliage and pale mauve flowers.

Polyantha rose 'The Fairy' underplanted with a purple *Ajuga reptans* variety (bugle).

An unusual but effective group, consisting of red climbing rose 'Amadis', yellow *Cytisus battandieri* and *Rosa moyesii*.

The lilacs, or varieties of *Syringa vulgaris,* are still flowering in June and could be combined with the earliest-flowering roses. For instance, try the pure white hybrid perpetual rose, 'Frau Karl Druschki', with purple or purplish red lilac. This rose has no scent but this essential ingredient will be provided by the lilac.

The mock orange or philadelphus is an 'essential' cottage- or country-garden shrub with its deliciously scented white flowers in early summer. It goes well with many roses, but particularly any with pink or red blooms which appear at this time of year, like the rose 'Common Moss'. This has very fragrant bright pink flowers which contrast beautifully in colour and shape with the mock orange.

Other shrubs which associate well with old-fashioned roses include the butterfly bushes or varieties of *Buddleia vulgaris,* which flower in late summer and autumn. Use the blue or purple varieties with red or pink roses, but choose roses which repeat later in the season; or better still those which have good crops of hips and/or autumn foliage colour, like the *rugosa* 'Frau Dagmar Hastrup'.

There are several perennials, too, which could be included in a late-summer/autumn group, like the Michaelmas daisies, especially varieties of *Aster amellus* with violet or lavender-blue flowers. The red-hot pokers or kniphofias with fiery orange, flame-coloured or cream flowers are at their best in late summer/autumn and are favourite cottage-garden perennials. In late summer the border phloxes come into bloom, varieties of *Phlox paniculata.* I particularly like white varieties of phlox with red or pink roses and suggest planting them in really bold groups to create impact.

Delphiniums, with bold spikes of blue, purple or white flowers in early summer are indispensable cottage-garden perennials and they contrast beautifully with the early summer roses in both colour and shape. Try some blue delphiniums, for instance, with the bourbon rose, 'Mme Isaac Pereire', which has beautifully fragrant purplish crimson flowers, the first of which appear in early summer.

The foxgloves, or digitalis, also have bold spikes of flowers which contrast well with old roses, but I would suggest a fairly modern strain such as the 'Excelsior Hybrids' in mixed colours. These come in with the early-flowering roses.

Also with tall bold spikes of flowers are the verbascums or mulleins. A great favourite with many people is the hybrid 'Gainsborough' which produces its 1.2 m (4 ft) spikes of light yellow flowers from early to late summer. It also has most attractive grey foliage and looks superb with pale pinks roses such as the alba rose, 'Great Maiden's Blush'.

Grey- or silver-leaved perennials go with all roses and two cottage-garden favourites are the artemisias, particularly the variety 'Lambrook Silver' with much-divided grey foliage and small grey flowers; and the catmints or nepetas, like *N. mussinii* (syn. *N. faassenii*), with aromatic greyish green leaves and summer spikes of lavender blue flowers. It has a semi-spreading habit and makes a good edging plant. There is a taller variety called 'Six Hills Giant'. Grey- and silver-leaved plants make an especially attractive foil for red or pink roses: try them with the bright crimson and white striped gallica rose called 'Rosa Mundi'.

A favourite combination of mine is the pale pink centifolia rose 'Fantin Latour' surrounded by red columbines or aquilegias, indispensable cottage-garden perennials. A particularly striking variety of aquilegia is 'Crimson Star' whose crimson and white flowers should overlap with those of 'Fantin Latour'.

Other favourite perennials are the hollyhocks, with their tall stems of rosette-like flowers in summer. The strain 'Chater's Double', with paeoni-like double flowers in various colours such as shades of pink, red, yellow and white, is superb planted with white roses, like the damask 'Mme Hardy', which has highly fragrant blooms in early and mid-summer. This combination looks marvellous near the front door of a cottage – the hollyhocks with the backing of the house wall, and the rose near the path so it can be easily sniffed!

These are just a few ideas for possible rose/

shrub/perennial combinations in cottage and country gardens – ideas which I have seen or tried. There is no end to possibilities and you really cannot go far wrong, provided you avoid colours which clash violently (such as brilliant orange-flowered perennials with shocking-pink roses!)

OLD GARDEN ROSES

Let us now consider some of the old-fashioned roses which would look very much at home in cottage and country gardens. I have selected from the hundreds available mainly those which are best known and most popular. Certainly all will provide an excellent show each year and hopefully you will not be disappointed with any of them. The old roses are catalogued into various groups, so I have followed this grouping in my descriptive lists. Planting distance is roughly equal to height.

The China roses

The middle of the eighteenth century saw the first China roses in gardens. They have a long flowering season (they are repeat-flowering). Many varieties were raised by rose breeders during the last century. They do not make very tall bushes – average height is around 1.2 m (4 ft) – and most have quite attractive glossy foliage.

'CÉCILE BRUNNER' This is probably the best known of the China roses and a great favourite with its tiny palest pink blooms appearing over a long period.

'OLD BLUSH CHINA' This variety bears sprays of semi-double, silvery pink blooms.

'PERLE D'OR' The buff-yellow flowers, shaded with pink, double and highly fragrant, are set against deep green foliage. It is a vigorous and easily grown variety.

The rugosa roses

These are noted for their disease resistance, having very healthy deep green foliage, and exceptionally prickly stems. Flowers may be single or double; many are well scented and the single-flowered varieties generally produce good crops of decorative hips in the autumn. All of those descibed are repeat-flowering, producing several flushes of blooms during the season.

'ALBA' A 1.8 m (6 ft) high shrub bearing big single scented blooms and large red hips. Good autumn foliage colour.

'BLANC DOUBLE DE COUBERT' A 1.8 m (6 ft) tall shrub bearing double fragrant white flowers over a very long period.

'PINK GROOTENDORST' Produces a profusion of small clear pink blooms. Height 1.2 m (4 ft).

'ROSERAIE DE L'HAY' Big crimson-purple blooms with a powerful fragrance. Also good autumn foliage colour. Height about 1.5 m (5 ft).

'RUBRA' This has large single mauvish pink blooms and colourful hips in the autumn.

'SARAH VAN FLEET' Highly fragrant, semi-double clear pale pink blooms. Height about 1.5 m (5 ft).

'SCABROSA' The large single flowers are velvety crimson-mauve and followed by large red hips. Height about 1.2 m (4 ft).

'SCHNEEZWERG' Pure white semi-double flowers with golden stamens. Long flowering season, the blooms being followed by crops of scarlet hips. Height about 1.2 m (4 ft).

The bourbon roses

These were first grown in the middle of the last century and have never lost their popularity. They are variable in habit of growth but are repeat-flowering.

'BOULE DE NEIGE' Strongly fragrant creamy white flowers are set against attractive shiny foliage. Flowers in summer and autumn. Height about 1.5 m (5 ft).

A country cottage traditionally has climbing roses around the front door. Here mellow Cotswold stone makes a superb background for these pale pink climbers.

Rosa longicuspis is a vigorous climber, seen here growing over a pergola, but it is also highly recommended for growing through large trees and conifers.

'HONORINE DE BRABANT'   This is an attractive striped rose, the flowers being lilac and purple and richly fragrant. Height 1.5–1.8 m (5–6 ft).

'LA REINE VICTORIA'   Cup-shaped blooms in deep lilac-pink set against good green foliage. Height about 1.5 m (5 ft).

'LOUISE ODIER'   Camellia-like double blooms in rose pink. Highly fragrant. Height 1.2 m (4 ft).

'MME ISAAC PEREIRE'   Large flowers, richly fragrant, in purplish crimson. A large vigorous shrub up to 1.8 m (6 ft) in height. This rose is suitable for training on a pillar or post. It can also be pruned hard each year if you desire a smaller shrub.

'MME PIERRE OGER'   Cup-shaped flowers in palest silvery pink, delightfully fragrant. Height about 1.2 m (4 ft).

'SOUVENIR DE LA MALMAISON'   Huge double quartered blooms in cream-pink with a deeper pink centre. Highly fragrant. Flowers spasmodically and does not do well in wet weather. Height about 3.6 m (12 ft). Perhaps best grown on a pillar.

'VARIEGATA DI BOLOGNA'   Cream-white striped with purple, and highly fragrant. Height around 1.8 m (6 ft).

Hybrid perpetual roses

First grown in the middle of the last century, the hybrid perpetuals are variable in habit but repeat in the autumn. Flowers may be double or single and the degree of fragrance varies from one variety to another. Some are tall vigorous shrubs, other are of low compact habit.

'FERDINAND PRICHARD'   Double flowers striped pink and crimson, on a bushy plant up to about 1.5 m (5 ft) in height.

'FRAU KARL DRUSCHKI'   A well-known variety with large pure white blooms without scent, borne on a large bush about 1.8 m (6 ft) in height.

'PAUL NEYRON'   Deep pink flowers, moderately scented. The huge blooms are shaped like those of paeonies. Height about 1.2 m (4 ft).

'REINE DES VIOLETTES'   Velvety violet flowers produced in early summer, with a few following later in the season. The blooms are well scented. Height is about 1.8 m (6 ft).

'ROGER LAMBELIN'   Double flowers in deep crimson striped with white and pink. The petals are attractively frilled and the blooms are fragrant. An eye-catching variety but needs careful cultivation: deserves cossetting. Height is around 1.2 m (4 ft).

'SOUVENIR DU DOCTEUR JAMAIN'   The superb flowers of this variety are purple, shaded with rich crimson, and deliciously fragrant. It is best grown in dappled shade so that hot sun does not ruin the blooms. Height is about 2.4 m (8 ft).

The alba roses

This group is very ancient, flowering in early summer, usually fragrant, and highly resistant to the rose diseases. They make very leafy bushes, with greyish green foliage providing a good background for the flowers. Of vigorous habit but suitable for small borders.

'CELESTIAL'   Semi-double flowers in light pink, contrasting well with the greyish foliage. A highly recommended variety which attains a height of around 1.8 m (6 ft).

'GREAT MAIDEN'S BLUSH'   Double, palest pink flowers, highly fragrant, set against bluish grey foliage. Height 1.5–1.8 m (5–6 ft).

'KÖNIGIN VON DÄNEMARK'   In English, 'Queen of Denmark'. The bright pink flowers are quartered and highly fragrant, set against pale grey-green foliage. Height 1.5–1.8 m (5–6 ft).

'MME PLANTIER'   Cream-white double flowers are produced in early summer. The tall stems will need some support, such as a pillar, or the plant can be trained to a wall. Height is at least 2.4 m (8 ft).

'MAXIMA'   This is popularly known as the Jacobite rose and bears double cream-white blooms. It's vigorous and large, attaining a height of about 2.4 m (8 ft).

The gallica roses

This group contains some of the oldest cultivated roses. They are not very prickly and make quite compact bushes. The single or double flowers are generally fragrant.

'BELLE DE CRÉCY' Virtually thornless, this rose has deliciously scented mauve and pink blooms in summer. Height is about 1.2 m (4 ft).

'CARDINAL DE RICHELIEU' Deep purple velvety flowers with tremendous fragrance. Compact habit of growth, attaining a height of about 1.2 m (4 ft).

'CHARLES DE MILLS' The double quartered blooms are a mix of purple and crimson and carried on a 1.2–1.5 m (4–5 ft) bush.

'COMPLICATA' In early summer this superb rose produces single flat blooms in bright pink with prominent yellow stamens. Quite thorny, with an arching habit of growth to about 2.4 m (8 ft) in height. Can either be grown as a free-standing shrub or trained to a pillar or wall.

'ROSA MUNDI' This is a very popular rose whose flowers are striped bright crimson and white and produced during early and mid-summer. Also known as *Rosa gallica versicolor*. It makes a bushy plant about 1.2 m (4 ft) in height.

The moss roses

These are favourite old roses, much loved by the Victorians. They have mossed flower-buds and stalks and are usually fragrant. Most rose colours are to be found in these roses. Some varieties are repeat-flowering, others producing only one flush of blooms in the summer. All of those described below are summer flowering.

'COMMON MOSS' The highly fragrant cup-shaped blooms are rose pink and heavily mossed. Height is 1.5–1.8 m (5–6 ft).

'NUITS DE YOUNG' The small double blooms are velvety blackish purple with golden stamens. Heavily mossed. Height about 1.2 m (4 ft).

'WHITE MOSS' Double flowers, heavily mossed, highly fragrant and pure white. Height about 1.5 m (5 ft).

'WILLIAM LOBB' The crimson-purple flat flowers have heavily mossed buds. It's a vigorous rose at about 1.8 m (6 ft) in height and is best supported.

The centifolia roses

Also known as cabbage roses, this ancient group is variable in habit and most varieties are very thorny. The flowering season varies but most varieties do not produce any more blooms after mid-summer. The fully double flowers are globular – perhaps cabbage-like, hence the alternative name for this group.

'BLANCHEFLEUR' The double highly fragrant blooms are white, but sometimes tinted with pink. Height is about 1.2 m (4 ft).

R. centifolia cristata This is also known as the crested moss rose but it is not a true moss rose, although the sepals do have some moss. The double flowers are rose pink. Another name for this rose is 'Chapeau de Napoléon'. Height is about 1.5 m (5 ft).

'FANTIN LATOUR' A well-known variety with cup-shaped pale pink flowers, fragrant, produced in profusion on a 1.5 m (5 ft) high bush.

The damask roses

Some damask roses are summer flowering and others repeat in the autumn. They have a delightful, very distinctive fragrance.

'ISPAHAN' The double pink flowers are produced over a long period and set against attractive glossy foliage. Height is about 1.2 m (4 ft).

'MME HARDY' This is one of the truly great damask roses, with pure white, highly fragrant double blooms. Height is about 1.5 m (5 ft).

'OMAR KHAYYAM' The rosette-like blooms are light pink and set against attractive grey foliage. Fragrant. Height from 1–1.5 m (3–5 ft).

Here an old dead tree has been turned into an attractive feature by growing a climbing rose up through it.

Delphiniums contrast beautifully with roses in colour and form. The red rose at the front of this pleasing group is floribunda 'Happy Wanderer'.

'YORK AND LANCASTER'   The flowers are striped with pale pink and white and carried on a large sprawling bush about 1.8 m (6 ft) in height. It needs a fertile soil to grow well.

ROSE HEDGES

In a country or cottage garden a rose hedge makes a good boundary, far more colourful than many other hedging plants. Or the garden could be divided by rose hedges to create that all-important element of surprise. A rose hedge could, perhaps, be used to screen the vegetable plot.

There are disadvantages as well as advantages with a rose hedge. The main disadvantage is that it is deciduous – it will drop its leaves in the autumn and look rather bare over winter. However, to compensate you will have lots of colour in the summer and you don't have to do a lot of trimming as rose hedges are grown informally. Indeed if you prune too hard you may not have such a floriferous hedge. Being informal, though, rose hedges tend to become rather on the wide side after a few years so you need a reasonable amount of space. The odd bit of pruning may be needed – to shorten any overlong shoots, for instance, and to cut out any dead wood. This is done in the winter or early spring. It pays to remove dead flower heads in the summer.

Rosa rugosa varieties are undoubtedly the best for hedging and especially in a country or cottage garden. They are animal-proof as the stems are very prickly, disease free and many produce colourful hips in the autumn to extend the season of colour.

If you want a hedge of 1.2 m (4 ft) high and over, the bushes should be planted 1 m (3 ft) apart in a line. For low hedges, say between 60 and 120 cm (2 and 4 ft) high, plant 45 cm (18 in) apart.

Recommended varieties

R. rugosa varieties: 'Alba', 'Rubra', Roseraie de l'Hay', 'Scabrosa' and 'Schneezwerg' are all highly recommended and described on page 49. In my opinion the absolute best of these are 'Roseraie de l'Hay' and 'Scabrosa'. All of these will make hedges between 1.2 and 2.4 m (4 and 8 ft) in height. Another good *rugosa* variety for hedging is 'Frau Dagmar Hastrup', with single clear rose pink flowers and good autumn leaf colour and hips. It will make a hedge between 60 and 120 cm (2 and 4 ft) in height.

Penzance hybrid sweet briars: 'Lady Penzance' and 'Lord Penzance' are two excellent roses for hedging in country or cottage gardens. Both have sweetly scented foliage. 'Lady Penzance' has single flowers in coppery pink and prominent yellow stamens. The blooms are followed by bright red hips. Lord Penzance' also has single blooms but they are buff-yellow touched with pink and are again followed by good crops of hips. Height of both varieties is 1.8 m (6 ft).

OLD CLIMBERS AND RAMBLERS

There are lots of delightful old climbers and ramblers for the cottage or country garden, for growing on walls, fences, arches, pergolas and the like. They can even be trained up posts of suitable height in a border if you do not have other supports.

Either grow them alone or let them intertwine with other old-fashioned climbers like honeysuckles, summer jasmine and clematis. If you only have a shady (for instance, north-facing) wall or fence you will find in the following list several varieties that will flourish and flower well in these conditions.

'ALBÉRIC BARBIER'   A favourite old rose suitable for a north wall. It's a summer-flowering rambler with double ivory flowers from cream-yellow buds. Attractive shiny foliage. Height about 4.5 m (15 ft).

'AMADIS'   A rambler with semi-double to double flowers in crimson purple carried in large clusters on reddish, thornless stems.

'CLIMBING CÉCILE BRUNNER' Summer flowering, with tiny soft pink fragrant blooms on a vigorous plant. Height about 7.6 m (25 ft).

'CRIMSON SHOWER' A fairly modern summer-flowering rambler but one which looks quite at home in a cottage garden. It has small crimson rosette-like flowers and shiny foliage. Height about 2.4 m (8 ft).

'DOROTHY PERKINS' Summer-flowering rambler with large clusters of small rose pink flowers. Very popular with cottage gardeners. Height about 3 m (10 ft). Unfortunately it is susceptible to rose mildew.

'GLOIRE DE DIJON' A repeat-flowering climbing tea rose with large well-scented flowers of buff-yellow shaded pink. Very popular; and vigorous, growing to 3.6 m (12 ft).

'MERMAID' A beautiful climber whose large pale yellow blooms have a boss of amber stamens, set against a background of attractive shiny foliage. It grows well on a north wall; and is vigorous once established, attaining a height of about 6 m (20 ft).

'MME ALFRED CARRIÈRE' Another climber suitable for a north wall; and very popular. It's repeat flowering and has small rounded white flowers with a touch of pink. They are highly fragrant. Height about 3.6 m (12 ft).

'MME GRÉGOIRE STAECHELIN' A very popular climber with hybrid-tea-type flowers in pale pink, deeper on the reverse. Well scented. Vigorous, to a height of about 4.5 m (15 ft).

'PAUL'S SCARLET' One of the most popular old summer-flowering ramblers, with large clusters of semi-double flowers in bright scarlet. Sometimes more blooms follow in autumn. Vigorous habit, to a height of about 3.6 m (12 ft).

'SEAGULL' This is an extremely vigorous rambler introduced at the beginning of this century. The single pure white flowers, each with a boss of golden stamens, are carried in large clusters. The plant can attain a height of 6 m (20 ft).

'YELLOW BANKSIAN' Also known as *Rosa banksiae lutea*. It has double pale yellow flowers in large clusters but, unfortunately, the display is over by early summer. Give it a sheltered sunny wall and it will make a specimen up to 4.5 m (15 ft) in height. No pruning should be done or you will lose flowers.

'ZÉPHIRINE DROUHIN' This is a highly popular thornless climber with very fragrant carmine-pink blooms which repeat. Height is about 3 m (10 ft). Suitable for growing on a north wall.

Old climbers and ramblers for trees

It is a fairly safe bet that many old country and cottage gardens have a large mature tree or two, or maybe a tall conifer. These make excellent supports for vigorous climbers and ramblers which will support themselves by twining among the branches. When a mature rose is in full flower in a tall tree it is a sight to behold. One of the most breathtaking effects I have seen was the white *Rosa filipes* 'Kiftsgate' growing through a tall dark green conifer (perhaps a variety of the Lawson cypress, *Chamaecyparis lawsoniana*). The deep green foliage made a superb background for the myriad small white rose blooms.

So let's take a look at some suitably vigorous climbers and ramblers.

'ALBERTINE' This is a well-known and highly popular old rambler which blooms in early and mid-summer. From copper-red buds come double salmon pink highly fragrant flowers. It is a vigorous variety and will soon reach a height of at least 4.5 m.

'FÉLICITÉ ET PERPÉTUÉ' This summer-flowering rambler has small double blooms in big clusters. The colour is cream and there is some scent. The foliage is almost evergreen. Very vigorous, soon attaining a height of 5.4 m (18 ft).

R. filipes 'KIFTSGATE' Growing to at least 9 m (30 ft) in height, this climber produces huge clusters of small white flowers in mid-summer. In my opinion there is no finer rose for growing up large trees and conifers.

'FRANÇOIS JURANVILLE' A summer-flowering rambler with salmon pink flowers. Height is about 6 m (20 ft).

A lovely idea for a cottage garden – stately foxgloves which contrast in shape with shrub roses 'Rainbow' and Cocktail'.

The vigorous rambler, 'Rambling Rector', growing through a large tree. It flowers in mid-summer.

R. longicuspis This has small white flowers, which have a fruity scent – if you can reach them! This vigorous climber can reach a height of at least 6 m (20 ft). The shiny foliage is almost evergreen.

'RAMBLING RECTOR' A good choice for a church-yard, perhaps? This rambler produces clusters of double white flowers in mid-summer. It is extremely vigorous and can attain a height of at least 6 m (20 ft).

'THE GARLAND' Small semi-double cream-white flowers produced in profusion during early and mid-summer. Highly fragrant. Vigorous habit to a height of about 4.5 m (15 ft).

'VEILCHENBLAU' Small semi-double violet-purple flowers are borne in large clusters. A good climber for shade when the colour of the flowers is preserved. Height is about 4.5 m (15 ft).

'WEDDING DAY' This rambler is summer flowering and has highly fragrant single pale yellowish white flowers in clusters. It is a modern variety but very much in keeping with country gardens. Very vigorous habit with an ultimate height of 7.6 m (25 ft).

6

GROUND COVER

It is only in comparatively recent times that the idea of completely covering the ground – for example on banks and around shrubs – with low-growing or prostrate plants has become popular with amateur gardeners. The idea of using ground-cover plants is to create labour-saving areas, for the dense growth suppresses annual weeds (but not perennials) and does away with the need for soil cultivation.

And it is only within the past few years that the use of roses for ground cover has aroused interest among private gardeners. There have been one or two ground-cover roses around for a long time but they were little used for the purpose. Now there is a wide range to choose from and many rose catalogues list a number of these varieties, most very new indeed.

The ground-cover roses have a prostrate, arching or bushy habit of growth, depending on variety, but all effectively cover the ground with a dense mass of weed-suppressing growth. They have a long season of interest: as well as flowers many produce attractive autumn hips and some have quite attractive foliage. All are extremely hardy and adaptable, tolerating poor soils and extreme environmental conditions. They need little or no pruning and due to their great vigour are extremely tolerant of pests and diseases.

Many rose nurserymen propagate ground-cover roses from cuttings so the gardener does not have problems from sucker growth.

You should choose ground-cover roses according to their vigour. For large-scale work there are extremely vigorous varieties, often with an arching habit, ideal for covering extensive banks, or other areas in a large garden where bold splashes of colour are required.

The less vigorous and more compact varieties are suited to small or medium-sized gardens and combine well with shrubs and herbaceous plants, say in a mixed border. They are recommended, too, for clothing banks.

Ground-cover roses are certainly among the most colourful plants for stabilizing soil, whether loose soil on a bank or light sandy soil which is being blown away by the wind.

I have indicated that ground-cover roses will perform well in poor soil conditions, but of course if you are able to improve the soil then the sooner you will achieve good and effective cover. It is important to eradicate all perennial weeds before planting.

The only pruning required is the removal of any old or dead growth – too much pruning will increase vigour but reduce flowering. Although most varieties are disease resistant it is advisable to spray against diseases and pests for the first couple of years after planting to help the plants establish quickly. Thereafter they will be able to cope on their own.

Recommended varieties of medium vigour

These are best for small and medium-sized gardens, for covering the ground around larger shrubs and groups of perennials, and for clothing banks.

'FERDY'   This has an arching habit of growth with well-textured foliage which stays on the plants until late in the autumn. It has small soft pink double flowers carried in large clusters: at their best in early

'Rosa Mundi' is a very popular old garden rose, which blooms during early and mid-summer. It is highly recommended for cottage and country gardens.

There is no better background for climbing roses than old mellow stone or brickwork.

summer but repeating in autumn. Planting distance is 90 cm (3 ft) apart each way.

'FIONA'   This has an arching, rambling habit of growth and deep green shiny foliage, an excellent background for the semi-double blood-red flowers which are produced from early summer. Great crops of colourful small hips are a feature in the autumn. Planting distance is 90 cm (3 ft) apart each way.

'FRAU DAGMAR HASTRUP'   An old *rugosa* variety with beautiful single pale rose-pink flowers, each with a boss of cream stamens. The flowers come from striking brilliant pink buds, and they repeat. Large round crimson hips are a feature in the autumn and winter. The habit of growth is bushy and recommended planting distance is 60 cm (2 ft) apart each way.

'HANSA'   Another *rugosa* variety of bushy habit. The highly fragrant flowers are of an unusual colour and fully double: they are reddish violet and produced all through the summer. In the autumn the large red hips come into their own. This variety is highly resistant to disease. Planting distance is 60 cm (2 ft) apart each way.

'MOJE HAMMARBERG'   Of bushy habit, this variety produces large double highly fragrant blooms in a shade of reddish violet and these are followed by big red hips. It is repeat flowering. Planting distance is 60 cm (2 ft) apart each way.

R. nitida   A species rose of bushy dense habit producing single bright pink flowers in summer. It is noted for its colourful autumn hips. Recommended planting distance is 60 cm (2 ft) apart each way.

'NOZOMI'   This was one of the first hybrid ground-cover roses to become popular and is still highly recommended. It has a prostrate habit of growth and is repeat flowering. The small single flowers are very pale pink and carried in large clusters. It will flower for a good eight weeks during the summer. Recommended planting distance is 60 cm (2 ft) apart each way.

'PINK BELLS'   A delightful variety with an arching habit of growth, well-covered with small deep green glossy leaves. The pale pink double blooms are carried in large clusters during mid- and late summer. Recommended planting distance is 90 cm (3 ft) apart each way.

'PINK DRIFT'   Of prostrate habit, this variety has attractive foliage and carries large clusters of small double pale pink blooms. Suggested planting distance is 90 cm (3 ft) apart each way.

'RED BELLS'   A highly recommended variety with an arching habit of growth. It is very much like 'Pink Bells', except that it has brilliant crimson-red blooms. Recommended planting distance is 90 cm (3 ft) apart each way.

'SNOW CARPET'   A compact prostrate variety – indeed, a miniature ground-cover rose. It is only 15 cm (6 in) high and spreads no more than 90 cm (3 ft). It is repeat-flowering, blooming from early summer to mid-autumn. The small double flowers are pure white. Recommended planting distance is 45 cm (1½ ft) apart each way.

'SWANY'   This variety has a prostrate habit of growth and repeats its small double white flowers, each flushed with pink at first. The small glossy leaves make a good background for the blooms. Recommended planting distance is 60 cm (2 ft) apart each way.

'THE FAIRY'   Bushy habit of growth, the plants being smothered with small double pink blooms in large clusters. It is repeat flowering and an old favourite. It is doubtful, though, whether it was originally used for ground cover. Hips are a feature in the autumn. Recommended planting distance is 60 cm (2 ft) apart each way.

'WHITE BELLS'   Virtually the same as 'Pink Bells', except that the double flowers are white. This arching plant should be set 90 cm (3 ft) apart each way.

Recommended vigorous varieties

'GROUSE'   Although only a few centimetres high, this variety can spread to 3 m (10 ft). It bears masses of single fragrant pale pink flowers during mid- and late summer. The shiny foliage is disease resistant. Recommended planting distance is 1.2 m (4 ft) apart each way.

'MAX GRAF' A hybrid *rugosa* with a prostrate habit, bearing in early and mid-summer bright pink single flowers each with a paler centre. They are strongly scented. Planting distance is 90 cm (3 ft) apart each way.

'PARTRIDGE' This has a similar habit of growth to 'Grouse' but the single flowers are pure white. Recommended planting distance is 1.2 m (4 ft) apart each way.

R. paulii A species of prostrate habit with masses of white, scented, starry flowers each with a conspicuous boss of golden stamens. Recommended planting distance is 1.2 m (4 ft) apart each way.

'PHEASANT' Prostrate habit of growth with big double flowers in large trusses, deep rose pink in colour and repeating. Planting distance 1.2 m (4 ft) apart each way.

'PINK WAVE' An arching habit of growth and double soft pink flowers in abundance from early summer to early autumn. Planting distance is 1.2 m (4 ft) apart each way.

'RED BLANKET' Arching habit of growth with semi-double rose-red blooms repeating throughout the season. Planting distance is 1.2 m (4 ft) apart each way.

'RED MAX GRAF' Of prostrate habit, this variety has large single flowers in bright crimson-scarlet, making a stunning display for much of the summer. Recommended planting distance is 1.2 m (4 ft) apart each way.

'ROSY CUSHION' Arching habit of growth with clusters of single rose-pink flowers each with a creamy centre. Repeat-flowering. Planting distance is 1.2 m (4 ft) apart each way.

'SMARTY' Of arching habit, a repeat-flowering variety with single pale pink blooms borne in clusters. Shiny foliage makes a good background for the flowers. Recommended planting distance is 1.2 m (4 ft) apart each way.

Other plants as companions

Ground-cover roses can of course be grown on their own if desired, planting maybe several varieties in bold groups or patches rather than single specimens. This patchwork effect looks particularly attractive on a bank.

Although ground-cover roses have a long season of interest there is, nevertheless, a large part of the year when they provide no interest at all. With some the hips may last into winter, it is true, but at that time further colour from other plants is desirable.

So consider using other ground-cover shrubs with the roses, again planting each in a bold group to create a patchwork of colour and texture. You will need to use the more vigorous ground-cover shrubs for this purpose as diminutive kinds would look completely out of place and could be partially smothered by the roses.

So let's concentrate on companion ground-cover shrubs for autumn, winter and spring colour and interest.

Some of the ground-cover cotoneasters can be recommended for autumn berries and, with some, leaf colour. *C. adpressus praecox* has arching branches laden with large orange-red berries in autumn. The hybrid 'Coral Beauty' has a wide-spreading habit, glossy evergreen leaves and orange-red berries. Then there's the ever-popular *C. horizontalis* with rich autumn leaf colour and masses of red berries. 'Hybridus Pendulus' can be grown as ground cover; it has evergreen foliage and a mass of brilliant red berries which are held well into winter. *C. salicifolius* 'Parkteppich' is a scrambling evergreen, semi-prostrate in habit, with lots of small red berries in autumn. The hybrid 'Skogholm' is a wide-spreading evergreen with small leaves and large coral-red fruits.

There's a ground-cover pyracantha or firethorn which I can highly recommend called 'Alexander Pendula'. Like other firethorns it has evergreen foliage and in the autumn smothers itself with small orange berries. It is a strong vigorous grower and so goes well with ground-cover roses.

'The Fairy' is a favourite old repeat-flowering rose with a bushy habit of growth which makes excellent ground cover. Here it contrasts beautifully with a variegated grassy aquatic at the edge of a pool.

'Nozomi' was one of the first ground-cover roses to become popular and is still highly recommended. It is of medium vigour, ideal for a small or medium-sized garden.

The evergreen ground-cover junipers really come into their own in the winter and spring when the roses are least attractive and devoid of leaves. The shore juniper, *Juniperus conferta,* has extremely prickly bright green foliage which presents a pleasing texture when mass planted. The *Juniperus × media* varieties make good companions for ground-cover roses, including 'Gold Sovereign' which has layers of bright yellow foliage; 'Hetzii' with tiers or layers of almost horizontal branches, a flattish habit and greyish green feathery foliage; 'Old Gold', similar habit but with greenish gold foliage; and 'Pfitzerana Aurea', the golden pfitzer juniper, with layers of horizontal branches clothed with yellow-green foliage which turns golden in summer. *J. sabina* 'Tamariscifolia' is a variety of savin juniper with a prostrate habit and feathery grey-blue foliage. *J. squamata* 'Meyeri' has a distinctive shape – the branches are held out at an angle of about 45 degrees. They are densely clothed with hard, prickly, steel-blue foliage. *J. virginiana* 'Grey Owl' is semi-prostrate and a strong grower, whose foliage has attractive greyish tints.

Grey foliage goes well with roses and while it shows up well in winter and spring it will not detract from the beauty of the roses in summer – indeed it enhances the effect. One of the best grey ground-covering shrubs for associating with roses is *Senecio* 'Sunshine', formerly known as *S. greyi.* This forms a dense mound of evergreen silvery grey foliage, covered with white felt below. In summer it produces yellow daisy flowers. When grown with roses I prefer to cut these off as they do not, in my opinion, look particularly attractive with rose blooms. There is another senecio that you could use instead – *S. laxifolius.* This is rather similar to 'Sunshine' but the leaves are smaller and more pointed. Also it is less hardy so not to be recommended for cold areas. It is excellent by the sea in mild areas.

A dwarf ground-covering form of the cherry laurel, *Prunus laurocerasus,* called 'Otto Luyken' goes well with roses and produces masses of white spiky flowers in spring, set against dark green evergreen foliage. It has a dense mounded habit of growth.

The woolly willow, *Salix lanata,* has a low spreading habit of growth and downy silvery-grey deciduous leaves which complement the flowers of the roses in summer. For spring interest it produces upright grey-yellow woolly catkins.

One of my favourite ground-cover plants for a bank is in fact a climber – the Virginia creeper, *Parthenocissus quinquefolia.* Grown as ground cover on a bank it will make a cascade of foliage which in autumn turns to fiery scarlet and orange shades, like molten lava flowing down among the roses, contrasting beautifully with any autumn blooms and with rose hips.

Of course you will want these ground-cover shrubs to form dense cover quickly so plant them fairly close together, much the same distance as the roses, that is, from 60 to 120 cm (2–4 ft) apart each way according to spread. The most vigorous plants are the parthenocissus, the cotoneasters, pyracantha and the junipers.

7

CARING FOR ROSES

One does not necessarily have to spend a great deal of time caring for roses to achieve good growth and flowering. For instance, many need virtually no pruning. The large-flowered, cluster-flowered, climbers and ramblers are most labour-intensive in respect of pruning.

Apart from pruning if necessary, feeding, watering and pest and disease control are the major aspects of care (but even the latter can be minimized if disease-resistant varieties are chosen).

It pays to get roses off to a good start by preparing the soil well and planting correctly. So let's start with these aspects.

SOIL PREPARATION AND IMPROVEMENT

I have considered soil types in Chapter 1 but it is a safe bet that all garden soils will benefit from some attention prior to planting roses.

Firstly there is digging of beds and borders. Deep digging is recommended, to two depths of the spade (known as double digging), to improve drainage and to enable the roses to root deeply, when they will find moisture in times of drought.

To double dig a bed or border, start at one end by taking out a 60 cm (2 ft) wide trench, the depth of the spade, across the plot. Deposit the soil near to where the final trench will be, at the other end of the plot.

Then get into the trench and dig the bottom to the depth of the spade (or use a fork if the soil is hard). There is no need to turn the soil over – just thoroughly break it up and loosen it.

Next take out another 60 cm wide trench immediately behind the first and throw the soil forward into the first trench, at the same time turning it over. Again get into the trench and break up the soil in the bottom. Continue in this way until the plot has been dug and fill the final trench with the soil taken from the first one.

It is advisable to eradicate all perennial weeds prior to digging, by treating them when they are in full growth with a weedkiller containing glyphosate. For perennial weed grasses, like couch, use a weedkiller containing alloxydim sodium.

Roses like plenty of bulky organic matter in the soil. This helps to conserve moisture in dry weather and improves the drainage of heavy clay soils. The best form of organic matter for roses is well-rotted farmyard manure. A good alternative is garden compost. Both supply plant foods. If you cannot obtain either, use spent mushroom compost, spent hops, peat or composted bark. None of these supplies much in the way of nutrients.

Add the organic matter during digging, spreading a layer in the bottom of each trench. A quarter of a barrowload will be sufficient for each 1.2 m (4 ft) length of trench. If you have a very poor shallow soil it would be a good idea to mix organic matter into the top 30 cm (12 in) as well.

About a week prior to planting break down the

roughly dug soil with a fork, at the same time incorporating a proprietary rose fertilizer or a general-purpose fertilizer. Firm the soil moderately by systematically treading with your heels all over the site.

PLANTING

Bare-root roses (those lifted from the grower's field) such as are supplied by mail-order specialists or bought pre-packed from a garden centre or

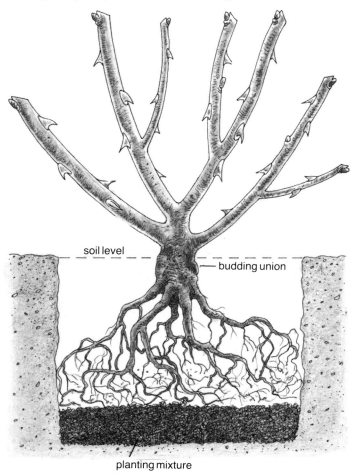

soil level

— budding union

planting mixture

supermarket, are planted during the dormant season, from late autumn until early spring. First trim back any damaged or broken roots, then plant in a hole sufficiently deep to allow the roots to stretch down to their full extent – do not allow any roots to turn upwards. Return fine soil around the roots, firming well with your heels as you proceed. After planting, the budding union – the swollen part right at the base of the stem – should be just below soil level (Fig. 7).

Container-grown roses bought from a garden centre can be planted at any time of year but most people like to buy and plant when they are in flower – choosing varieties which appeal in respect of colour, scent, etc. The container must be removed exceedingly carefully so as not to disturb the soilball. The latter must be moist when planting, so stand the container in a bucket of water beforehand if the compost is drying out. Take out a hole only slightly wider and deeper than the soilball, set the latter centrally in the hole and return fine soil in the space all round, firming with your heels. Again make sure the budding union is just below soil level.

A word about planting mixtures. These are highly recommended, especially if you have a poor soil, as they help the roses to establish quickly. Use a proprietary planting mixture or make your own – a 9 litre (2 gallon) bucketful of peat with a handful of sterilized bonemeal well mixed in. Mix a few handsful into the soil in the bottom of the planting hole and with the soil which is to be returned.

PRUNING

Pruning after planting

Newly planted large-flowered and cluster-flowered roses should be pruned in the early spring. Prune the

Fig. 7. *Left:* Planting a bare-root rose. Note that the budding union is just below soil level and the roots have been well spread out. Planting mixture worked into the bottom of the hole ensures rapid establishment.

stems really hard, even though they will have been cut back by the nurseryman prior to dispatch. All stems can be reduced to a height of 15 cm (6 in) above soil level. Very thin or spindly shoots should be removed at the same time.

All pruning cuts should be about 5 mm ($\frac{1}{4}$ in) above *outward-facing* growth buds, and the cuts should slant slightly away from the buds. This applies to regular pruning, too, described below.

Routine pruning

The large-flowered and cluster-flowered roses, climbers and ramblers are the only groups of roses which need annual pruning.

The large-flowered roses are pruned in early spring. The aim is to produce an open-centred or cup-shaped bush consisting only of strong stems. Strong stems are cut back by half to two-thirds of their length; weaker ones to 5–8 cm (2–3 in). Weak or spindly stems or shoots are removed completely (Fig. 8).

The cluster-flowered roses are pruned at the same time of the year and in virtually the same way. Strong stems are cut back by one-third to half their length; weaker ones by two-thirds. Again, all weak and spindly stems and shoots are removed completely.

The large-flowered and cluster-flowered standard roses are pruned as described above (one prunes the head of branches, of course). Do ensure, though, that all remaining branches are of the same length. This gives a nice symmetrical head (Fig. 9).

Climbing roses are pruned in early spring, too. All the side shoots are cut back to leave one to three growth buds (Fig. 10).

Rambler roses are pruned immediately after flowering. They make new shoots near the base, which will flower in the following year. The old stems which have flowered are cut out completely and the new shoots tied in to their supports.

Wherever possible the majority of stems of climbing and rambler roses should be tied in horizontally, as this encourages side shoots to be freely produced and hence more flowers. This is not possible when training roses to pillars and similar supports. In this instance the roses will produce most flowers near the tops of the stems.

Climbers and ramblers must be tied in securely to their supports to prevent winter gales from lashing them around and causing damage. Tarred string is best as it lasts for a number of years.

Dead-heading

Dead flower heads should be removed from repeat-flowering roses – those that produce several flushes of blooms – as it encourages more blooms to follow. Do not remove them, though, from roses which produce attractive hips in the autumn, or these will not then be formed.

When removing dead blooms cut off the complete flower stalk as well, to just above a growth bud. Use a pair of secateurs to make really clean cuts.

Occasional pruning

The other groups of roses really need no pruning apart from the removal of dead and dying shoots or stems. This can be done in the winter. Extremely old wood can be thinned out, the aim always being to leave as much young wood as possible. Any overlong stems can be judiciously shortened. The same comments apply to rose hedges.

Sucker removal

Suckers are vigorous shoots which grow from the rootstock of budded roses. The shoots therefore occur below the budding union of the plants and generally grow from the roots. You will notice that the leaflet shape and colour are different from those of the variety.

Suckers should be removed as they are very

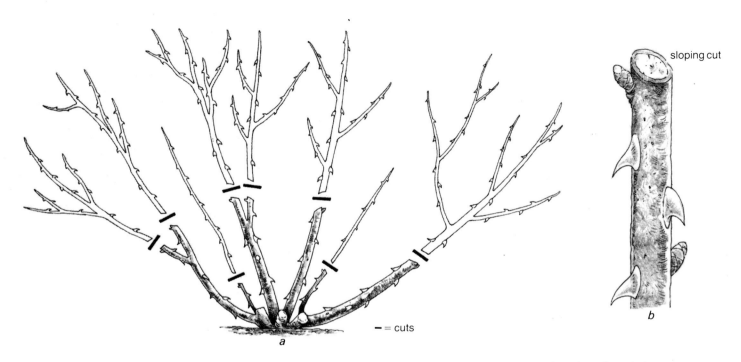

Fig. 8. Pruning a large-flowered bush rose. Reduce strong growths to half to two-thirds of their length, and weak shoots to 5 – 7.5 cm (2 – 3 in). Always cut to outward-facing buds.

vigorous and will soon swamp the plant. On no account cut them off at ground level or this will result in many more being produced. Instead trace the suckers to their point of origin by scraping away the soil. Then wrench them out (Fig. 11). Replace the soil and firm it well. If any suckers are produced on the stems of standard roses they should be rubbed out at an early stage of their development.

GENERAL CARE

Feeding

Roses are greedy plants – or should we say that they respond favourably to regular and generous feeding.

You cannot do better than use a proprietary rose fertilizer, which should be applied according to the manufacturer's instructions. Use a granular fertilizer (as opposed to a liquid feed).

The first feed should be given in mid-spring. Another feed should be given after the first flush of blooms. Even feed again those roses which have only one flush per year.

Ideally the fertilizer should be lightly hoed into the soil surface when it will quickly become available to the plants. However this may not be possible if you have other plants growing around the roses, or have a permanent mulch (see below). In these instances just sprinkle the fertilizer on the surface.

If in the summer the roses seem to be in need of a boost, you could give them a foliar feed, using a proprietary product.

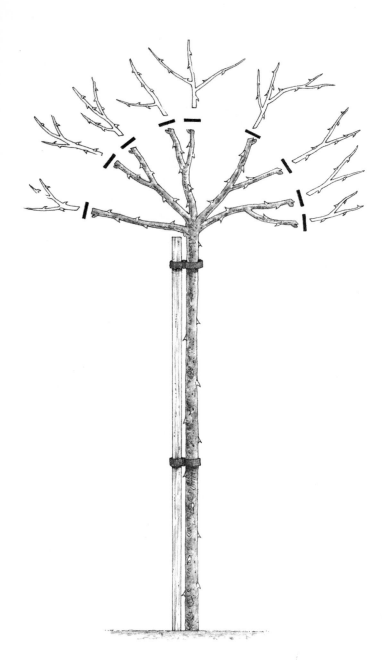

Mulching

A mulch is a layer of bulky organic matter spread over the surface of the soil around plants. Its purpose is to conserve soil moisture during dry spells and to suppress the growth of annual weeds. It is highly recommended for roses if you do not have other plants covering the ground around them.

The best mulching material for roses is undoubtedly well-rotted farmyard manure. Second best is well-rotted garden compost. Both supply plant foods, too. Other materials, which do not have any food value, include peat, chipped bark, partially composted bark, mushroom compost and spent hops.

A mulch is best laid in the spring, and topped up at this time annually, if necessary. The ground must be moist and weed free when laying a mulch. The depth should be between 5 and 8cm (2 and 3in). Do not allow the mulch to touch the stems of the roses.

Weed control

If you have bare soil around roses annual weeds will be a problem. They are best controlled by hoeing in the seedling stage on a warm dry day, when they will quickly dry up and die.

Alternatively you can use paraquat weedkiller among roses, provided you do not allow it to come into contact with the foliage. Use a watering can fitted with a dribble bar. If the odd perennial weed appears spot-treat it with glyphosate weedkiller.

Another way of keeping annual weeds under control is to sprinkle propachlor granules over the soil surface, which must be moist and completely weed free. This weedkiller will prevent the germination of weed seeds for up to eight weeks. The soil surface must not be disturbed after the application.

Fig. 9. Pruning a standard rose. The large-flowered and cluster-flowered kinds are pruned in the same way as bushes, but all the remaining branches should be of the same length to ensure a symmetrical head.

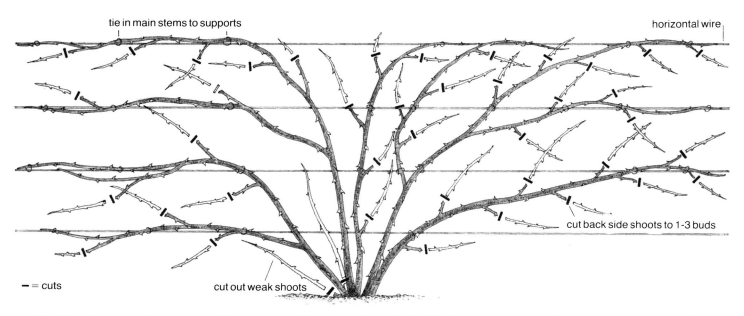

tie in main stems to supports

horizontal wire

cut back side shoots to 1-3 buds

— = cuts

cut out weak shoots

Fig. 10. Pruning a climbing rose. These are pruned in early spring. All the side shoots are cut back to leave one to three growth buds. Remove completely any weak shoots. Tie in main stems to supports.

Watering

It is essential to water roses well in dry periods in the spring and summer, if the soil starts to dry out, as it will keep them growing and flowering.

As soon as the top inch or so has dried out you should apply water. The aim should be to keep the top 15 cm (6 in) moist. You should therefore apply enough water each time for it to penetrate at least 15 cm (6 in) deep and this means the equivalent of 2.5 cm (1 in) of rain. This amounts to about 27 litres of water per m² (4¾ gallons per square yard). This amount of water is best applied by means of a sprinkler attached to a hosepipe. You can check the depth of penetration about an hour after watering by digging a test hole 15 cm (6 in) deep with a hand trowel. If the soil is moist at the bottom you know you have applied sufficient water.

Newly planted roses are especially susceptible to dry conditions so keep these well watered. Of course, there may be restrictions on the use of water during drought conditions but if you use a mulch soil moisture will be conserved. Remember that the soil will dry out more rapidly if other plants are grown around the roses, as there will be more competition for moisture.

PESTS AND DISEASES

Some roses, particularly many of the shrub roses, are not troubled by diseases, and quite a few of the highly bred bush roses and climbers have a high degree of resistance. Nevertheless rose diseases can occur and as soon as noticed steps should be taken to control them.

Roses cannot be resistant to pests, but if they are well grown and healthy they will be better able to cope with attacks. However you should not allow pests to build up and as soon as any are observed you should, as with diseases, use an appropriate spray to control them.

Below I have listed and described some of the most common pests and diseases which can attack roses and have given methods of control. Hopefully you will not have all of them in your garden!

Diseases

BLACK SPOT A serious disease, but less of a problem in industrial and city areas. Appears as black spots on the leaves; a bad attack can result in leaf drop (Fig. 12). Remove and burn affected leaves and spray with a combined rose spray, propiconazole or benomyl.

CANKER Sunken brown areas on stems, usually near the base. Cut out infected stems and burn.

MILDEW Rose mildew is one of the major rose diseases and appears as white powdery deposits on the leaves, buds and shoot tips. It can cause leaf fall and distortion. Spray with a combined rose spray or propiconazole.

RUST Orange pustules appear on the undersides of the leaves. Spray with mancozeb, propiconazole, or a bupirimate and triforine mixture.

SOIL SICKNESS If roses have been grown in the same bed for a decade or more the soil can become rose-sick. While the established roses are not affected, newly planted roses may fail to establish. This is commonly known as replant disease. Exactly what causes this problem has not yet been fully confirmed. However if you intend planting new roses in an old rose bed then you should first remove the topsoil from the planting site and replace with fresh topsoil which has not been used for roses.

Pests

APHIDS Greenfly or aphids are the most common pests of roses, clustering around shoot tips and buds and sucking the sap, causing a weakening effect. They multiply rapidly if not controlled by spraying with a combined rose spray, malathion, dimethoate, or a mix of permethrin and heptenophos.

sucker

Fig. 11. Suckers are vigorous shoots which grow from the rootstock of budded roses. To remove them, clear soil to expose their bases, then wrench them out.

Fig. 12. Rose black spot is a serious disease but less of a problem in industrial and city areas. A bad attack can result in leaf drop.

CAPSID Green bugs which feed on buds and young leaves, causing small buds to die and brown spots on leaves. Control as for aphids.

CATERPILLARS The caterpillars of various moths eat holes of irregular shape in the leaves.

Control by hand picking or by spraying with a combined rose spray.

COCKCHAFER A large reddish brown beetle which eats ragged holes in the leaves. Other chafer beetles eat the flowers. Best to pick off and destroy the beetles, which are not usually present in large numbers.

FROGHOPPER This is commonly known as cuckoo-spit, for it appears as white froth on shoots and stems. Inside the froth lives a yellow pest known as a froghopper, which feeds on the shoots. Either remove by hand, or wash off the froth with a hosepipe, then spray with an insecticide containing gamma-HCH.

LEAF-CUTTER BEE This cuts out neat holes around the edges of the leaves and takes them away. It is not often necessary to carry out control as damage is not usually extensive.

LEAFHOPPER The leafhopper is a small yellowish insect whose feeding habits result in pale mottling on leaves. Severe attack can result in leaf-fall. Spray with malathion, dimethoate, or a mix of permethrin and heptenophos.

LEAF-ROLLING SAWFLY Grey-green caterpillars roll up the leaves tightly and live inside, feeding on the foliage. Pick off by hand as soon as seen or spray with fenitrothion.

ROSE SLUGWORM A greenish yellow grub eats away the tissue between leaf veins, resulting in a skeletonized appearance. Spray with a mixture of permethrin and heptenophos, or dimethoate.

THRIPS These tiny insects can cause mottled and distorted foliage and flowers. Spray with malathion, fenitrothion, dimethoate, or a mixture of permethrin and heptenophos.

NOTE: A combined rose spray is a mixture of fungicides and insecticides which controls a wide range of rose diseases and pests. It saves using many different sprays. Several companies supply combined rose sprays.

APPENDIX

The Royal National Rose Society

The Royal National Rose Society was founded in 1876 for all who love roses. It has a growing membership, not only in the UK but in many countries worldwide.

The Society has a great collection of roses in its world-famous Gardens of the Rose at St Albans in Hertfordshire. These gardens contain 30 000 roses of some 1700 different varieties, ranging from the species through the historic and old-fashioned groups to the modern garden roses. There are trial grounds, too, at the Gardens. New varieties are sent there from all over the world to undergo a comprehensive three-year assessment. The aim of the trials is to assess new roses for their value as garden plants. They are judged weekly during the flowering season and the winners receive Society awards.

Each year in July the British Rose Festival is held at the Gardens: a great and spectacular attraction.

The Gardens are being continuously developed, in particular by associating roses with a great many other plants to create greater interest for visitors and to stimulate ideas leading to more adventurous gardening.

Membership of the RNRS gives you:
- The quarterly journal, *The Rose*
- Society handbooks on varieties and how to grow roses
- Entry to the Gardens of the Rose
- Entry to the British Rose Festival and to the Society's many other shows across the country
- An expert advisory service on all rose problems
- Use of world's most comprehensive rose library.

Full details of membership are available from the Secretary, The Royal National Rose Society, Chiswell Green, St Albans, Hertfordshire AL2 3NR.

INDEX OF ROSE VARIETIES AND SPECIES

A selection of rose specialists

Between them, the following rose specialists can supply all of the roses I have recommended. It is suggested that you send for their catalogues.

Anderson's Rose Nurseries
Cults
Aberdeen AB1 9QT

David Austin Roses
Bowling Green Lane
Albrighton
Wolverhampton WV7 3HB

Peter Beales Roses
London Road
Attleborough
Norfolk NR17 1AY

Cants of Colchester
The Old Rose Gardens
London Road
Stanway
Colchester
Essex CO3 5UP

James Cocker and Sons
Whitemyres
Lang Stracht
Aberdeen

Fryer's Roses
Knutsford
Cheshire WA16 0SX

Gandy's Roses
North Kilworth
Lutterworth
Leicestershire LE17 6HZ

Gregory's Roses
The Rose Gardens
Stapleford
Nottingham NG9 7JA

R. Harkness and Co.
The Rose Gardens
Hitchin
Hertfordshire SG4 0JT

LeGrice Roses
Norwich Road
North Walsham
Norfolk NR28 0DR

John Mattock
Nuneham Courtenay
Oxford OX9 9PY

Rearsby Roses
Melton Road
Rearsby
Leicester LE7 8YP

Rosemary Roses
The Nurseries
Stapleford Lane
Toton
Beeston
Nottingham NG9 5FD

Roses du Temps Passé
Woodlands House
Stretton
Near Stafford ST19 9LG

Sealand Nurseries
Sealand
Chester
Cheshire CH1 6BA

Warley Rose Gardens
The Garden Centre
Warley Street
Great Warley
Brentwood
Essex CM13 3JH

Wheatcroft Roses
Edwalton
Nottingham NG12 4DE